NEW ESSENTIAL

Writer's

COMPANION

HOUGHTON MIFFLIN COMPANY

BOSTON · NEW YORK

Visit our website: www.houghtonmifflinbooks.com

ISBN-13: 978-0-618-83705-2
ISBN-10: 0-618-83705-1

Manufactured in the United States of America

Book design by Catherine Hawkes, Cat & Mouse

QWB 10 9 8 7 6 5 4 3 2 1

CONTENTS

A GUIDE TO *Style*

A GUIDE TO *Writing*

A GUIDE TO
Style

Capitalize the following.

1. The first word of a sentence:

   > Some spiders are poisonous; others are not.
   > Are you the next in line?

2. The first word of a direct quotation, except when the quotation is split:

   > Joan asked, "Was the lecture interesting?"
   > "No," I responded, "it was very boring."
   > "The sublime and the ridiculous are often so nearly related,"
   > wrote Tom Paine, "that it is difficult to class them separately."

3. The first word of each line in a poem in traditional verse:

   > Half a league, half a league,
   > Half a league onward,
   > All in the valley of Death
   > Rode the six hundred.
   >   —*Alfred, Lord Tennyson*

4. Names of people, organizations and their members, councils and congresses, and historical periods and events:

   > Helen Keller
   > Albert Einstein
   > Benevolent and Protective Order of Elks
   > an Elk
   > Roman Catholic Church
   > a Catholic
   > Republican Party
   > a Republican
   > Interstate Commerce Commission
   > the US Senate
   > Department of Homeland Security
   > Middle Ages
   > World War II
   > Great Plague
   > Battle of Midway

5. Names of places and geographic divisions, districts, regions, and localities:

Arlington	Continental Divide
Wyoming	Middle East
Ukraine	Sunbelt
Fifth Avenue	Gulf States
Golden Gate Bridge	East Coast
Arctic Circle	Great Plains
Eastern Hemisphere	the Southwest

Do not capitalize words indicating compass points unless a specific region is referred to:

Turn north onto Interstate 91.
but
I grew up in the North but recently moved to the East.

6. Names of rivers, lakes, mountains, and oceans:

Nile River	Cascade Mountains
Lake Erie	Atlantic Ocean

7. Names of ships, aircraft, satellites, and space vehicles:

USS Arizona	*Spirit of St. Louis*
Voyager II	the space shuttle *Endeavor*

8. Names of nationalities, peoples, and languages:

Spanish	Sioux
Maori	Hindustani

9. Words derived from proper names, except in extended senses:

Byzantine Empire
but
byzantine office politics

10. Words indicating family relationships when used with a person's name as a title:

Aunt Helen and Uncle Thomas
but
my aunt and uncle, Helen and Thomas Ward

11. Titles, including civil, judicial, military, royal, noble, religious, and honorary titles, that precede a name:

Justice Thomas	Lord Mountbatten
General Bradley	Pope John Paul II

| Mayor Daley | Professor Jacobson |
| Queen Elizabeth | Senator Navarro |

12. Key words in titles of literary, dramatic, artistic, and musical works:

>the novel *The Great Gatsby*
>the short story "Notes from Underground"
>an article entitled "The Year in Review"
>Robert Frost's poem "The Road Not Taken"
>the play *Sunrise at Campobello*
>the movie *The Lion in Winter*
>Van Gogh's *Wheat Field and Cypress Trees*
>Beethoven's *Emperor Concerto*

13. The first word in the salutation or complimentary close of a letter:

| Dear Katherine, | Yours sincerely, |

14. Epithets and substitutes for the names of people and places:

| Old Hickory | the Oval Office |
| Old Blood and Guts | the Windy City |

15. Words used in personifications:

>When is not Death at watch
>Within those secret waters?
>What wants he but to catch
>Earth's heedless sons and daughters?
>　　　　　　　—*Edmund Blunden*

16. Names of deities and sacred works:

God	Supreme Being
Jehovah	Bible
Allah	Hebrew Scriptures
Osiris	New Testament
Zeus	Koran

17. Days of the week, months of the year, holidays, and holy days:

Tuesday	Passover
May	Ramadan
Independence Day	Christmas

18. Names of specific law courts:

Supreme Court of the United States
United States Court of Appeals for the First Circuit
Roxbury District Court

19. Names of treaties, pacts, laws, and amendments to the US Constitution:

Treaty of Westphalia Treaty of Paris
Geneva Accords Warsaw Pact countries
Sherman Antitrust Law Fourteenth Amendment

20. Registered trademarks and service marks:

Prozac Grammy

21. Names of geologic eras, periods, epochs, and strata and the names of prehistoric divisions:

Paleozoic Era Age of Reptiles
Precambrian Iron Age
Pleistocene Stone Age

22. Names of galaxies, constellations, planets, and stars:

Milky Way Jupiter
Southern Crown Polaris

23. Genus names in binomial nomenclature and names of classes, families, and all groups higher than genera:

Rana pipiens
Nematoda

Do not capitalize derivatives from such names:

nematode

Note that the species name is not capitalized, even when used alone:

The species *pipiens* is a member of the Ranidae family.

24. Many abbreviations and acronyms:

Dec. MFA
Lt. Gen. AIDS

25. Names of awards and prizes:

Nobel Prize Pulitzer Prize

ITALICS

Use italics for:

1. Titles of books, plays, magazines, newspapers, and epic poems:

    Animal Farm   *War and Peace*
    As You Like It   *Newsweek* magazine
    Gourmet   New York *Daily News*
    Wall Street Journal *Iliad*

2. Titles of movies and radio and television programs:

    The Lion King   *All Things Considered*
    Inherit the Wind   *Masterpiece Theatre*
    I Love Lucy

3. Titles of major musical compositions:

    Handel's *Messiah*
    Tchaikovsky's *Swan Lake*

4. Names of paintings and sculpture:

    Mona Lisa   *Pietà*

5. Words, letters, or numbers that are referred to as such:

    The word *hiss* is onomatopoeic.
    You form your *n*'s like *u*'s.
    A *6* looks like an inverted *9*.

6. Foreign words and phrases not yet assimilated into English:

    C'est la vie was the response to my complaint.

7. Names of the plaintiff and defendant in legal citations:

    Marbury v. *Madison*

8. Names of genera, species, subspecies, and varieties in botanical and zoological nomenclature:

    Homo sapiens
    Brassica oleracea var. *italica*

9. Names of ships, aircraft, satellites, and space vehicles:

    USS *Constitution*   *Spirit of St. Louis*
    Sputnik   *Enterprise* shuttle

Compound nouns

1. Compounds nouns may be open (written as two words), hyphenated, or solid (written as one word), and often more than one style is acceptable.

   attorney-at-law
   byproduct *or* by-product
   great-grandparent
   grownup *or* grown-up
   fundraiser *or* fund-raiser
   goodwill *or* good will
   lifestyle *or* life-style *or* life style

   If the compound in question cannot be found in a dictionary, write it as two words unless a hyphen is needed for clarity. When a noun that is an open compound is preceded by an adjective, a hyphen is often added to prevent confusion.

   costume designer; best costume-designer
   broom closet; tiny broom-closet
   desk lamp; large desk-lamp

2. Compound nouns consisting of a noun and a gerund are generally open. However, many such compounds have become solid, and when in doubt it is best to consult a dictionary.

   crime solving
   house hunting
   trout fishing
   faultfinding
   housekeeping

3. A compound consisting of two nouns of equal importance should be hyphenated.

   priest-king
   secretary-treasurer
   city-state
   singer-songwriter

Compound modifiers

1. Compound nouns used attributively should be hyphenated if there is any possibility of misreading. Adjectives beginning with *high*– or *low*– are generally hyphenated.

   > fine-wine tasting
   > hot-water bottle
   > minimum-wage worker
   > rare-book store
   > real-life experiences
   > hot-spot volcano
   > night-school students
   > high-school teacher
   > high-quality programming
   > low-budget films
   > low-res scan

   If there is no possibility of misreading, or if the hyphen would look clumsy, it may be omitted.

   > organic chemistry class
   > hedge fund manager
   > small claims court
   > mechanical engineering degree
   > bubonic plague outbreak
   > temp agency employee

   Names of chemical substances used as adjectives should not be hyphenated.

   > carbon monoxide poisoning
   > dichromic acid solution

2. A compound modifier consisting of an adverb ending in *–ly* plus a participle or an adjective should not be hyphenated.

   > a finely tuned mechanism
   > a carefully worked canvas
   > a skillfully written screenplay
   > the slowly moving train
   > a highly motivated student
   > unusually mild weather
   > an especially pleasant evening
   > a completely hopeless case

3. A compound modifier consisting of an adverb that does not end in *–ly* plus a participle or an adjective is hyphenated when it precedes a noun.

> a well-known actor
> an ill-advised move
> best-loved poems
> a much-improved situation
> a so-called cure
> less-expensive options

Such a compound is not hyphenated when it follows a noun unless it appears hyphenated in the dictionary.

> Nicole's essay was the best organized.
> His art was less appreciated back then.
> The house was well designed.
> They are well-known in Paris.

4. A compound modifier consisting of a noun or adjective plus a participle is hyphenated when it precedes the noun it modifies.

> helium-filled balloons
> thirst-quenching drink
> bone-chilling tale
> good-looking sons
> long-lasting friendship

Compounds of this type may be left open when they follow a noun unless they appear hyphenated or solid in the dictionary.

> The drink was thirst quenching.
> That job will be time-consuming.
> She remained tongue-tied.
> The consequences are far-reaching.
> The noise was earsplitting.

5. A compound modifier consisting of an adjective plus a noun to which *–d* or *–ed* has been added is hyphenated when it precedes a noun. It is best to consult a dictionary if in doubt as some of these compounds have become solid.

yellow-eyed cat
fine-grained wood
many-tiered cake
stout-limbed toddler
kindhearted person

Leave such compounds open when they follow a noun unless they are hyphenated or solid in the dictionary.

The child is rosy cheeked.
Our boss is even-tempered.
That hat is old-fashioned.
I was feeling lightheaded.

Color

1. Compound color adjectives are hyphenated.

    a red-gold sunset
    a cherry-red sweater
    blue-green eyes

2. Color compounds whose first element ends in *–ish* are hyphenated when they precede the noun but open when they follow the noun.

    a darkish-blue color
    a reddish-gold sunset
    The sky is reddish gold.
    My car is a darkish blue.

Phrases

1. Phrases used as modifiers are normally hyphenated.

    a happy-go-lucky person
    a here-today-gone-tomorrow attitude
    a fire-and-brimstone lecture

2. A foreign phrase used as a modifier is not hyphenated.

    a bona fide offer
    a per diem allowance

Proper names

1. Compound modifiers formed of capitalized words should not be hyphenated.

   Korean War veterans
   New Jersey shore
   Old English poetry
   Iron Age manufacture
   New World plants

2. Usage is divided with regard to compounds designating a nationality or ethnic group. It is generally unnecessary to hyphenate such terms whether used as nouns or adjectives. However, with some exceptions, compounds of this type frequently appear with hyphens.

   Native Americans; Native American nations
   Latin Americans; Latin American countries
   Italian Americans; Italian American neighborhood
   French Canadians; French-Canadian ancestry
   Mexican Americans; Mexican-American community
   African Americans *or* African-Americans
   African American literature *or* African-American literature
   Asian Americans *or* Asian-Americans
   Asian American studies *or* Asian-American studies

Numbers and measurements

1. A hyphen punctuates the compound numbers from 21 through 99 when they are written out.

   thirty-five students
   at age ninety-two
   four hundred eighty-six dollars

2. Compound modifiers with a numerical first element are generally hyphenated.

   second-rate movie
   seven-minute miles
   three-hour tour
   third-story window
   ten-thousand-year-old bones
   100-yard dash

13-piece band
19th-century novel
four-odd years
60-odd chairs

If, however, the second element is an abbreviated unit of measurement, the hyphen is omitted.

500 mL beaker
10 g mass

3. Spelled-out numbers used with *–fold* are not hyphenated; figures and *–fold* are hyphenated.

tenfold
20-fold

4. Spelled-out fractions used as nouns may be either open or hyphenated.

He ate seven eighths [*or* seven-eighths] of the pizza.
Three quarters [*or* Three-quarters] of the students are English majors.
Two thirds [*or* Two-thirds] is plenty.

When used as adjectives or adverbs, however, fractions are generally hyphenated.

She owns a three-fourths interest.
The refrigerator is four-fifths empty.
I am two-thirds finished with this assignment.

Prefixes

1. Normally, prefixes are joined to a second element without a hyphen unless doing so would double the same vowel.

antianxiety
anticrime
antiwar
anti-intellectual
anti-inflammatory
anti-infective

However, many common prefixes, such as *co–*, *de–*, *pre–*, and *re–*, are added without a hyphen even though a double vowel is the result.

coordinate	preestablish
cooperate	reenter
preeminent	reelect

2. A hyphen is used if the element following a prefix is capitalized or is a numeral.

anti-Semitism
pro-French
un-American
non-Germanic
pre-1900

3. The hyphen is usually retained in words that begin with *all–*, *ex–* (meaning "former"), *half–*, and *self–*.

all-around
ex-governor
half-baked, half-life *but* halfhearted, halfcocked, halfpenny,
halftone, halfway, half dollar
self-defense *but* selfhood, selfish, selfless, selfsame

4. Terms that begin with *quasi–* are hyphenated if used as adjectives and open if used as nouns.

quasi-scientific research
quasi-stellar object
quasi-judicial proceedings
a quasi success
a quasi corporation

5. Some prefixes are followed by a hyphen to prevent a misunderstanding of meaning.

re-form [compare *reform*]
re-cover [compare *recover*]
re-create [compare *recreate*]
re-lease [compare *release*]

Other uses

1. A hyphen indicates that two or more compounds share a single base.

six- and seven-year-olds
three- and four-volume sets
low- and high-range models
lower- and uppercase letters
pre- and postseason practice
first-, second-, and third-class mail

2. Nouns or adjectives consisting of a short verb combined with a preposition are either hyphenated or written solid depending on current usage. The same words used as a verb are written separately:

a breakup *but* break up a fight
a bang-up job *but* bang up the car

3. A hyphen indicates that a word has been divided at the end of a line of text.

Anatole France's actual name was Jacques Anatole Thibault.

Apostrophe

Use an apostrophe with the letter *s* or an apostrophe alone to indicate:

1. The possessive case of singular and plural nouns, indefinite pronouns, and surnames combined with designations such as *Jr.*, *Sr.*, and *II*:

   > my brother's wife
   > my three sisters' husbands
   > They answer each other's phones.
   > John Smith, Jr.'s, car

2. Joint possession when used with the last of two or more nouns in a series:

   > Mary and Peter's report

3. Individual possession or authorship when used with each of two or more nouns in a series:

   > Smith's, Roe's, and Doe's reports

4. Plurals of words, letters, or figures when this is not clear without the apostrophe:

   > the 60's and 70's   *x*'s, *y*'s, and *z*'s
   > *but*
   > the 1920s   TVs

5. Omission of letters in contractions:

   > aren't   o'clock

6. Omission of figures in dates:

   > the class of '63

Brackets

Use brackets to enclose:

1. Words or passages in quoted matter written by someone other than the author:

> A tough but nervous, tenacious but restless race [the Yankees]; materially ambitious, yet prone to introspection.
>
> —*Samuel Eliot Morison*

2. Material inserted within matter already in parentheses:

   (Arlington [VA], January 1, 2003)

Colon

Use a colon to:

1. Introduce words, phrases, or clauses that explain, amplify, or summarize what has gone before:

   > There are two cardinal sins from which all others spring: impatience and laziness.
   >
   > —*Franz Kafka*

   > Suddenly I realized where we were: London.

2. Introduce a long quotation:

   > In his original draft of the Declaration of Independence, Jefferson wrote: "We hold these truths to be sacred and undeniable; that all men are created equal and independent, that from that equal creation they derive rights inherent and inalienable."

3. Introduce a list:

   > We need the following items: pens, notepads, calendars, six pairs of scissors, and two rulers.

4. Separate chapter and verse numbers in biblical references:

   > James 1:4

5. Separate the hour and minutes in time designations:

   > 9:30 AM   a 9:30 meeting

6. Follow the salutation in a business letter:

   > Ladies and Gentlemen:

Comma

Use a comma to separate or set off:

1. Clauses of a compound sentence connected by a coordinating conjunction:

> There is a difference between the novels of Hemingway and Fitzgerald, and it is a difference worth noting.

Omit the comma in short compound sentences:

> I understand your argument but I do not agree.

2. The conjunction *and* or *or* from the preceding item in a series of three or more:

> The salad included lettuce, scallions, tomatoes, and radishes.

3. Two or more adjectives modifying the same noun if *and* could be used between them without altering the meaning:

> a solid, heavy gas
> *but*
> a polished mahogany dresser

4. Nonrestrictive clauses or phrases (i.e., those that would not affect the meaning of the sentence if eliminated):

> The burglar, who had entered through the patio, went straight to the silver chest.

The comma should not be used when a clause is restrictive (i.e., essential to the meaning of the sentence):

> The burglar who had entered through the patio went straight to the silver chest; the other burglar searched for the wall safe.

5. Words or phrases in apposition to a noun or noun phrase:

> Plato, the Greek philosopher, was a student of Socrates.

The comma should not be used if such words or phrases precede the noun:

> The Greek philosopher Plato was a student of Socrates.

6. Transitional words or short expressions that require a pause in reading or speaking:

> Oddly, my friend was not at home when I called.

7. Words used to introduce a sentence:

No, I haven't been to Houston.
Well, what do you think we should do now?

8. A subordinate clause or long phrase that precedes a principal clause:

   By the time we got home, we were tired.

9. Short quotations and sayings:

   "Talking of axes," said the Duchess, "chop off her head!"
   —*Lewis Carroll*
   The candidate said, "Actions speak louder than words."

10. The year from the month in full dates:

    Kennedy was assassinated on November 22, 1963.

    Note that no comma is used when only the month and the year are given:

    Kennedy was assassinated in November 1963.

11. The city and state in geographic names:

    Atlanta, Georgia, is the transportation center of the South.

12. A series of four or more figures into thousands, millions, etc.:

    82,000   300,000

13. Words used in direct address.

    I tell you, folks, all politics is applesauce.
    —*Will Rogers*
    Thank you for your help, Kevin.

14. A query from the rest of a sentence:

    You forgot your pass again, didn't you?

15. Sentence elements that could be misunderstood if the comma is not used:

    Some time after, the actual date for the project was set.

16. Titles and degrees from surnames and from the rest of a sentence:

    Susan P. Green, MD
    Joanne Henderson, PhD

Gregory A. Rossi, SJ
Harold T. Jones, Jr., presented the evidence.

Dash

Em dash. The most common dash is the em dash, so called because it is roughly the same width as a capital *M* in the typeface being used. Use an em dash to indicate or set apart:

1. A sudden break or abrupt change in continuity:

   "If—if you'll just let me explain—" the student stammered. The problem—if there really is one—can be solved if we discuss it.

2. An explanatory, defining, or emphatic phrase:

   Foods rich in complex carbohydrates and fiber—bread, cereal, rice, and pasta—should be eaten every day.

3. Parenthetical material or statements:

   Wolsey, for all his faults—and he had many—was a great statesman.

   —*Jasper Ridley*

4. An unfinished sentence:

   "But if my train is late—" she began.

5. A summarizing phrase or clause:

   The vital measure of a newspaper is not its size but its spirit—that is its responsibility to report the news fully, accurately, and fairly.

   —*Arthur H. Sulzberger*

6. The name of an author or source, as at the end of a quotation:

   A poet can survive everything but a misprint.
   —*Oscar Wilde*

En dash. The en dash is half the length of the em dash but longer than the hyphen. Use an en dash to indicate or set apart:

1. Numbers and words when the meaning is *through*, *to*, or *from . . . to*.

The years 2000–2004 were politically divisive.
Eva Perón (1919–52) was born to a poor family in Buenos Aires.
For tomorrow, please complete exercises 4–10 on pages 232–233.
The New York–Madrid flight is full.
We are open Monday–Friday, 9:00 AM–5:30 PM.

Do not use an en dash if the first number is preceded by the word *between* or *from*. Instead use *and*, *to*, or *through*.

Between 1953 and 1957 my parents lived in Jackson Heights.
The reception will be from 5:30 to 7:30.
From January 15 through March 31, Brian will be in
St. Augustine.

2. A compound adjective when one of the elements consists of two words.

the pre–Civil War era
a Pulitzer Prize–winning novel

Ellipses

Use ellipses to indicate omissions:

1. Three spaced points for the omission of words or sentences within quoted matter:

Equipped by education to rule in the nineteenth century . . . he lived and reigned in Russia in the twentieth century.
—*Robert K. Massie*

2. Four spaced points for the omission of words at the end of a sentence:

The timidity of bureaucrats when it comes to dealing with . . . abuses is easy to explain . . . .
—*New York*

Exclamation point

Use an exclamation point at the end of an emphatic or exclamatory sentence or statement:

Go home at once!
You must be kidding!
Bravo!

Parentheses

Use parentheses to enclose:

1. Material that isn't essential to a sentence and if not included would not alter its meaning:

   After a few minutes (some say less) the fire was extinguished.

2. Letters or figures that indicate subdivisions of a series:

   A movement in sonata form consists of the following elements: (1) the exposition, (2) the development, and (3) the recapitulation.

3. Figures that follow and confirm written-out numbers, especially in legal and business documents:

   Our estimate for the restoration work is six thousand dollars ($6,000).

4. An abbreviation for a term following the written-out term, when used for the first time in a text:

   The patient is suffering from severe acute respiratory syndrome (SARS).

Period

Use a period after:

1. A complete declarative or mild imperative sentence:

   There could be no turning back as war's dark shadow settled irrevocably across the continent of Europe.
   —*W. Bruce Lincoln*
   Return the books after you have finished reading them.
   Please sign here.

2. A sentence fragment:

   Gray clouds. A brisk wind. An icy sidewalk. Winter.

3. Some abbreviations:

   Dec.
   St.
   Blvd.
   Co.

Question mark

Use a question mark to:

1. Punctuate a direct question:

> Have you seen the new edition yet?
> Who's there?

A question mark is not used after indirect or implied questions:

> I wonder who said "Nothing is easy."
> I asked if they planned to leave.

2. Indicate uncertainty:

> Ferdinand Magellan (1480?–1521)
> Plato (427?–347 BC)

Quotation marks

Use double quotation marks (" ") to enclose:

1. Direct quotations:

> "What was New York like in the eighties?" our son asked.
> "Ladies and gentlemen," the announcer said, "the President of the United States."
> Robert Louis Stevenson said that it is "better to be a fool than to be dead."

2. Words or phrases that translate a foreign word or phrase:

> *ami*, "friend"   *die Grenze*, "the border"

3. Titles of articles in publications, essays, short stories, poems, songs, and short musical pieces:

> the article "How to Buy Spices"
> Pushkin's "The Queen of Spades"
> Teasdale's "There Will Come Soft Rains"
> Schubert's "Death and the Maiden"

Use single quotation marks to enclose quotations within quotations:

> "'We, the people' . . . is a very eloquent beginning."
> —*Barbara Jordan*

Put commas and periods inside quotation marks; put semicolons and colons outside. Other punctuation, such as exclamation points and question marks, should be put inside the closing quotation marks only if part of the matter quoted.

Semicolon

Use a semicolon to separate:

1. Clauses of a compound sentence having no coordinating conjunction:

   > Do not let us speak of darker days; let us rather speak of sterner days.
   >
   > —*Winston Churchill*

2. Clauses of a compound sentence in which the clauses contain internal punctuation, even when the clauses are joined by conjunctions:

   > Skis in hand, we trudged to the lodge, stowed our lunches, and donned our boots; and the rest of our party waited for us at the lift.

3. Elements of a series in which items already contain commas:

   > Among those at the diplomatic reception were the Secretary of State; the daughter of the Ambassador to the Court of St. James, formerly of London; and two United Nations delegates.

4. Clauses of a compound sentence joined by a conjunctive adverb, such as *however*, *nonetheless*, or *hence*:

   > Justin and I insisted on leaving as soon as possible; however, the rest of the group refused.

   A semicolon may also be used instead of a comma to signal longer pauses, as for dramatic effect:

   > But I want you to know that when I cross the river my last conscious thought will be of the Corps; and the Corps; and the Corps.
   >
   > —*General Douglas MacArthur*

Slash

Use a slash to:

1. Separate successive divisions in an extended date:

   fiscal year 2005/06

2. Represent the word *per*:

   1,800 ft/sec   35 km/hr

3. Substitute for the word *or* between the words *and* and *or*:

   Take water skis and/or fishing equipment when you visit the beach this summer.

4. Separate two or more lines of poetry that are quoted and run in on successive lines of a text:

   The student had a memory lapse upon reaching the lines "Double, double, toil and trouble / Fire burn and cauldron bubble / Eye of newt and toe of frog / Wool of bat and tongue of dog" and suddenly ran off the stage.

Although it would be impossible to formulate a set of rules that would cover the spelling of all English words, the seven basic rules given here are intended as an aid in learning and understanding the correct spelling of a large number of English words.

Seven basic rules of spelling

1. Adding a suffix to a one-syllable word.

   a. Words of one syllable that end in a single consonant preceded by a single vowel double the final consonant before a suffix beginning with a vowel: *bag, baggage; hop, hopper; red, redder; stop, stopped.* There are two notable exceptions to this rule: *bus* (*buses* or *busses; busing* or *bussing*) and *gas* (*gasses* or *gases; gassing; gassy*).

   b. If a word ends with two or more consonants or if it ends with one consonant preceded by two or more vowels instead of one, the final consonant is not doubled: *debt, debtor; lick, licking; mail, mailed; sweet, sweetest.*

2. Adding a suffix to a word with two or more syllables.

   a. Words of two or more syllables that have the accent on the last syllable and end in a single consonant preceded by a single vowel double the final consonant before a suffix beginning with a vowel: *admit, admitted; confer, conferring; control, controller; regret, regrettable.* There are a few exceptions: *chagrin, chagrined; transfer, transferred, transferring* but *transferable, transference.*

   b. When the accent shifts to the first syllable of the word after the suffix is added, the final consonant is not doubled: *prefer, preference; refer, reference.*

   c. If the word ends with two consonants or if the final consonant is preceded by more than one vowel, the final consonant is not doubled: *perform, performance; repeal, repealing.*

   d. If the word is accented on any syllable except the last, the final consonant is not doubled: *develop, developed; market, marketed.* However, some words like *cobweb, handicap,* and *outfit* follow the models of *web, cap,* and *fit,* even though these words may not be true compounds. A few others ending in *g* double the final *g* so that it will not be pronounced like *j: zigzag, zigzagged.*

3. Adding a suffix beginning with a vowel to a word ending in a silent *e*. Words ending with a silent *e* usually drop the *e* before a suffix beginning with a vowel: *force, forcible; glide, gliding; operate, operator; trifle, trifler.* However, there are many exceptions to this rule:

   a. Many words of this type have alternative forms: *blamable* or *blameable; bluish* or *blueish.* And in certain cases, alternative forms have different meanings: *linage* or *lineage* (number of lines) but *lineage* (ancestry).

   b. Many words ending in *ce* or *ge* keep the *e* before the suffixes *–able* and *–ous: trace, traceable; advantage, advantageous.*

   c. Words ending in a silent *e* keep the *e* if the word could be mistaken for another word: *dye, dyeing; singe, singeing.*

   d. If the word ends in *ie,* the *e* is dropped and the *i* changed to *y* before the suffix *–ing.* A word ending in *i* remains unchanged before *–ing: die, dying; ski, skiing.*

   e. *Mile* and *acre* do not drop the *e* before the suffix *–age: mileage, acreage.*

4. Adding a suffix beginning with a consonant to a word ending in a silent *e*. Words ending with a silent *e* generally retain the *e* before a suffix that begins with a consonant: *plate, plateful; shoe, shoeless; arrange, arrangement; white, whiteness.* However, there are many exceptions to this rule. Some of the most common are: *abridge, abridgment; acknowledge, acknowledgment; argue, argument; awe, awful; due, duly; judge, judgment; nine, ninth; true, truly; whole, wholly; wise, wisdom.*

5. Adding a suffix to a word ending in *y*.

   a. Words ending in *y* preceded by a consonant generally change the *y* to *i* before the addition of a suffix, except when the suffix begins with an *i: accompany, accompaniment; beauty, beautiful; icy, icier, iciest, icily, iciness;* but *reply, replying.*

b. The *y* is retained in derivatives of *baby*, *city*, and *lady* and before the suffixes *–ship* and *–like*: *babyhood*, *cityscape*, *ladyship*, *ladylike*.

c. Adjectives of one syllable ending in *y* preceded by a consonant usually retain the *y* when a suffix beginning with a consonant is added: *shy, shyly, shyness; sly, slyly, slyness; wry, wryly, wryness;* but *dryly* or *drily, dryness.* These adjectives usually also retain the *y* when a suffix beginning with a vowel is added, although most have variants where the *y* has changed to *i: dry, drier* or *dryer, driest* or *dryest; shy, shier* or *shyer, shiest* or *shyest.*

d. Words ending in *y* preceded by a vowel usually retain the *y* before a suffix: *buy, buyer; key, keyless; coy, coyer, coyest; gay, gayer, gayest;* but *day, daily; gay, gaily* or *gayly.*

e. Some words drop the final *y* before the addition of the suffix *-eous: beauty, beauteous.*

6. Adding a suffix to a word ending in *c*. Words ending in *c* almost always have the letter *k* inserted after the *c* when a suffix beginning with *e*, *i*, or *y* is added: *panic, panicky; picnic; picnicker.*

7. The problem of "*ie*" or "*ei*."

a. When the two letters have a long *e* sound (as in *feet*), *i* generally comes before *e*, except after *c: believe, chief, grieve, niece, siege, shield;* but *either, leisure, neither, seize, sheik.*

b. After *c*, *e* generally comes before *i: ceiling, conceit, deceive, perceive, receive, receipt;* but *ancient, financier, specie.*

c. When the two letters have a long *a* sound (as in *cake*), a short *e* sound (as in *pet*), a short *i* sound (as in *fit*), or a long *i* sound (as in *mine*), *e* generally comes before *i: Fahrenheit, foreign, forfeit, height, neighbor, sleight, sovereign, surfeit;* but *friend, handkerchief, mischief, sieve.*

Many words spelled with *ie* or *ei* present no difficulties because the vowels are pronounced separately: *deity, piety.*

Forming plurals

1. The plural of most nouns is formed by adding *s* to the singular: *apples, epochs, griefs, months, Georges, the Romanos.*

2. a. Common nouns ending in *ch* (soft), *sh*, *s*, *ss*, *x*, *z* or *zz* usually form their plurals by adding *es*: *churches, slashes, gases, classes, foxes, buzzes.*

b. Proper nouns of this type add *es*: *Charles, the Charleses; the Keaches; the Joneses; the Coxes.*

3. a. Common nouns ending in *y* preceded by a vowel usually form their plurals by adding *s*: *bays, guys, keys, toys.*

b. Common nouns ending in *y* preceded by a consonant or by *qu* change the *y* to *i* and add *es*: *baby, babies; city, cities; faculty, faculties; soliloquy, soliloquies.*

c. Proper nouns ending in *y* form their plurals regularly, and do not change the *y* to *i* as common nouns do: *the two Kathys; the Connallys; the two Kansas Citys.* There are a few well-known exceptions to this rule: *the Alleghenies, the Ptolemies, the Rockies, the Two Sicilies.*

4. Most nouns ending in *f*, *ff*, or *fe* form their plurals regularly by adding *s* to the singular: *chief, chiefs; proof, proofs; roof, roofs; sheriff, sheriffs; fife, fifes.* However, some nouns ending in *f* or *fe* change the *f* or *fe* to *v* and add *es*: *calf, calves; elf, elves; half, halves; knife, knives; life, lives; loaf, loaves; self, selves; shelf, shelves; thief, thieves; wife, wives; wolf, wolves.* A few nouns ending in *f* or *ff*, including *beef, dwarf, hoof, scarf, wharf,* and *staff* have two plural forms: *beefs* or *beeves; dwarfs* or *dwarves; hoofs* or *hooves; scarfs* or *scarves; wharfs* or *wharves; staffs* or *staves.* In this case, sometimes different forms have different meanings, as *beefs* (complaints) and *beeves* (animals) or *staffs* (people) and *staves* (long poles).

5. a. Nouns ending in *o* preceded by a vowel form their plurals by adding *s* to the singular: *cameos, duos, studios, zoos.*

b. Most nouns ending in *o* preceded by a consonant also usually add *s* to form the plural: *altos, casinos, egos, Latinos.* However, some nouns ending in *o* preceded by a consonant add *es*: *echoes, heroes, jingoes, noes, potatoes, tomatoes.* Some nouns ending in *o* preceded by a consonant have two plural forms: *buffaloes* or *buffalos; cargoes* or *cargos; desperadoes* or *desperados; halos* or *haloes; mosquitoes* or *mosquitos; zeros* or *zeroes.*

6. Most nouns ending in *i* form their plurals by adding *s: alibis, khakis, rabbis, skis.* Three exceptions are *alkali, taxi,* and *chili: alkalis* or *alkalies; taxis* or *taxies; chilies.*

7. **a.** A few nouns undergo a vowel change in the stem: *foot, feet; goose, geese; louse, lice; man, men; mouse, mice; tooth, teeth; woman, women.* Usually compounds in which one of these nouns is the final element form their plurals in the same way: *webfoot, webfeet; gentleman, gentlemen; dormouse, dormice; Englishwoman, Englishwomen.* Note, however, that *mongoose* and many words ending in *man,* such as *German* and *human,* are not compounds. These words form their plurals by adding *s: mongooses; Germans, humans.*

   b. Three nouns have plurals ending in *en: ox, oxen; child, children; brother, brothers* (of the same parent) or *brethren* (a fellow member).

8. **a.** Compounds written as a single word form their plurals the same way that the final element of the compound does: *cloths, dishcloths; brushes, hairbrushes; wives, midwives; men, anchormen; women, businesswomen.*

   b. In rare cases both parts of the compound are made plural: *manservant, menservants.*

   c. Compounds ending in *–ful* normally form their plurals by adding *s* at the end: *cupfuls, handfuls, tablespoonfuls.*

   d. Compound words, written with or without a hyphen, that consist of a noun followed by an adjective or other qualifying expression form their plurals by making the same change in the noun as when the noun stands alone: *daughter-in-law, daughters-in-law; man-of-war, men-of-war; heir apparent, heirs apparent; notary public, notaries public.*

9. Some nouns, mainly names of birds, fishes, and mammals, have the same form in the plural as in the singular: *bison, deer, moose, sheep, swine.* Some words that follow this pattern, such as *antelope, cod, crab, elk, fish, flounder, grouse, herring, quail, reindeer, salmon, shrimp,* and *trout,* also have regular plurals ending in *-s: antelope, antelopes; fish, fishes; salmon, salmons.* Normally in such cases the unchanged plural denotes that the animal in question is being considered collectively, while the plural ending in *s* is used specifically to

denote different varieties or species or kinds: *We caught six fish* but *Half a dozen fishes inhabit the lake*. By far, however, most animal names take a regular plural: *dogs, cats, lions, monkeys, whales*.

10. **a.** Many words indicating nationality or place of origin have the same form in the plural as in the singular: *Japanese, Milanese, Swiss*.

   b. Similarly a few names of tribes or peoples have the same form in the plural as in the singular: *Iroquois; Sioux*. Many other such names have both an unchanged plural form and a regular plural form ending in *s*: *Apache* or *Apaches; Cherokee* or *Cherokees; Eskimo* or *Eskimos; Zulu* or *Zulus*.

11. Many nouns derived from a foreign language retain their foreign plurals: (from Latin) *alumna, alumnae; bacillus, bacilli; genus, genera; series, series*; (from Greek) *analysis, analyses; basis, bases; crisis, crises; criterion, criteria* or *criterions; phenomenon, phenomena* or *phenomenons*; (from French) *adieu, adieux* or *adieus; beau, beaux* or *beaus; madame, mesdames*; (from Italian) *paparazzo, paparazzi*; (from Hebrew) *cherub, cherubim* or *cherubs; kibbutz, kibbutzim*. As you can see, many words of this type also have a regular plural ending in *s* or *es*, in which case the English plural is usually the one used in everyday speech, and the foreign plural is reserved for a technical sense or for use by a specialist: *antennas* (TV or radio part) or *antennae* (physiological structure).

12. **a.** Usage with regard to forming the plurals of letters, numbers, and abbreviations varies. Generally, if the term consists of two or more characters, add *s*: *the ABCs, the 1980s, PhDs, several IOUs*. If the term consists of a single character, use *'s*: *three A's, p's and q's, I's, 2's*.

   b. The plural of a word being used as a word is indicated by *'s*: *underline all the* but's.

Word compounding

A compound word is made up of two or more words that together express a single idea. There are three types of compound words. An *open compound* consists of two or more words written separately, such as *salad dressing* or *April Fools' Day*. A *hyphenated compound* has words connected by a hyphen, such as *mother-in-law* or *force-feed*. A *solid compound* is two words that are written as one word, such as *keyboard* or *typewriter*. In addition, a compound may be classified as permanent or temporary. A *permanent compound* is fixed by common usage and can usually be found in the dictionary, whereas a *temporary compound* consists of two or more words joined by a hyphen as needed, usually to modify another word or to avoid ambiguity. The following general rules apply to forming compounds.

Prefixes and suffixes

1. Normally, prefixes and suffixes are joined with a second element without a hyphen, unless doing so would double a vowel or triple a consonant: *antianxiety, anticrime, antiwar* but *anti-intellectual; childlike, taillike* but *bell-like*. Even so, many common prefixes, such as *co-, de-, pre-,* and *re-,* are added without a hyphen although a double vowel is the result: *coordinate, preeminent, reenter.*

2. A hyphen is also used when the element following a prefix is capitalized, or when the element preceding a suffix is a proper noun: *anti-American, America-like.*

3. The hyphen is usually retained in words that begin with *all-, ex-* (meaning "former"), *half-, quasi-* (in adjective constructions), and *self-: all-around; ex-governor; half-life* but *half-hearted, halfpenny, halftone, halfway; quasi-scientific* but *a quasi success; self-defense* but *selfhood, selfish, selfless, selfsame.*

4. Certain homographs require a hyphen to prevent mistakes in pronunciation and meaning: *recreation* (enjoyment), *re-creation* (new creation).

When the compound is a noun or adjective

5. In order to avoid confusion, compound modifiers are generally hyphenated: *fine-wine tasting; high-school teacher; hot-water bottle; minimum-wage worker; rare-book store; real-life experiences.* If there is no possibility of confusion, or if the hyphen would look clumsy, omit the hyphen: *bubonic plague*

outbreak, chemical engineering degree, temp agency employee.

6. When a noun that is an open compound is preceded by an adjective, the compound is often hyphenated to avoid confusion: *wine cellar, damp wine-cellar; broom closet, tiny broom-closet; house cat, old house-cat.*

7. Compound adjectives formed with *high-* or *low-* are generally hyphenated: *high-quality programming; low-budget films.*

8. Compound adjectives formed with an adverb plus an adjective or a participle are often hyphenated when they occur before the noun they modify: *a well-known actor, an ill-advised move, best-loved poems, a much-improved situation, the so-called cure.* However, when these compounds occur after the noun, or when they are modified, the hyphen is usually omitted: *the actor is well known; an extremely well known actor.* Many compounds of this type are permanent hyphenated compounds: *a well-done steak; the steak was well-done.*

9. If the adverb ends in *–ly* in an adverb-adjective compound, the hyphen is omitted: *a finely tuned mechanism; a carefully worked canvas.*

10. Compound adjectives formed with a noun and a past participle are always hyphenated when they precede the noun they modify: *helium-filled balloons, snow-capped mountains.* Many compounds of this type have become permanent and are hyphenated whether they precede or follow the noun they modify: *the tongue-tied winner; She remained tongue-tied.*

11. Also hyphenate compound adjectives formed with an adjective and a noun to which *–d* or *–ed* has been added: *yellow-eyed cat, fine-grained wood, many-tiered cake, stout-limbed toddler.* Many such compounds have become permanent hyphenated or solid compounds: *middle-aged, old-fashioned, lightheaded, kindhearted.*

12. Compound adjectives formed with a noun, adjective, or adverb and a present participle are hyphenated when the compound precedes the noun it modifies: *a bone-chilling tale, two good-looking sons, long-lasting friendship.* Many such compounds have become permanent solid compounds:

earsplitting, farseeing. Many such compounds have become permanent and are hyphenated whether they precede or follow the noun they modify: *far-reaching consequences; The consequences are far-reaching.*

13. Compound nouns formed with a noun and a gerund are generally open: *crime solving, house hunting, trout fishing.* Many such compounds, however, have become permanent solid compounds: *faultfinding, housekeeping.*

14. Compound modifiers formed of capitalized words should not be hyphenated: *Old English poetry; Iron Age manufacture; New World plants.*

15. Usage is divided with regard to compounds that are proper names used to designate ethnic groups. Under normal circumstances such terms when used as nouns or adjectives should appear without a hyphen: *a group of African Americans, many Native Americans, French Canadians in Boston; a Jewish American organization, Latin American countries.* However, many (but not all) compounds of this type are now frequently hyphenated: *African-Americans, French-Canadian music.*

16. Nouns or adjectives consisting of a short verb and a preposition are either hyphenated or solid depending on current usage. The same words used as verbs are written separately: *a breakup* but *break up a fight; a bang-up job* but *bang up the car.*

17. Two nouns of equal value are hyphenated when the person or thing is considered to have the characteristics of both nouns: *secretary-treasurer, city-state, time-motion study.*

18. Compound forms must always reflect meaning. Consequently, some compounds may change in form depending on how they are used: *Anyone may go* but *Any one of these will do; Everyone is here* but *Every one of these is good.*

19. Scientific compounds are usually not hyphenated: *carbon monoxide poisoning; dichromic acid solution.*

When should a number be spelled out and when should it be written in figures? In cases in which the following rules do not apply, the choice is determined by the kind of document you are writing; numbers are customarily written out in formal writing and figures employed in informal writing and business writing. As with many areas covered in this book, consistency of style is paramount. Whatever method you use, stick with it throughout.

Numbers from one to ten are spelled out, and numbers over ten are written in figures:

> There are five candidates running for the council.
> We received 17 letters inquiring about the job.

Indefinite and round numbers are spelled out:

> The college president received hundreds of angry calls.
> They drove five hundred miles yesterday.
> Management and staff agreed to a sixty-forty split of the profits.

Definite amounts and long numbers are written in figures:

> They paid $183,000 for the house.
> She won the election by 759,323 votes.
> The pistachio nuts are $12.95 a pound.

Numbers in the millions and above, however, are written in either figures or words and followed by *million* or *billion*:

> The population of the island nation is nearly 47 million.
> The house and stables cost four and a half million dollars.
> The company was awarded a three-billion-dollar contract.

Two or more related numbers in the same sentence should be expressed in the same style; if one of the numbers is greater than ten, all should be expressed in figures:

> Today he typed 4 reports, 11 memos, and 7 letters.
> There were 25 players trying out for 10 spots on the team.

Spell out numbers at the beginning of a sentence:

> Three shipments arrived today.
> Seventy-five percent of the inventory was damaged.

If this produces too great an inconsistency within the sentence or produces too unwieldly a sentence, you can either break the related numbers rule or rewrite the sentence so that the number does not come first:

> Five people applied for the 12 positions.
> We received 5 applications for the 12 positions.
> Forty-five hundred acres were planted in corn.
> Corn was planted in 4,500 acres.

Unrelated numbers in the same sentence should be distinguished for clarity. Figures and words can be used to differentiate them:

> In three days, we sold 24 cars, 6 campers, and 11 trucks.
> State records for the second quarter indicate 0.7 inches of rainfall, 25 sunny days, and a temperature range of 45–98°F.

Unrelated numbers should not be placed next to each other when written as figures. You can spell out one of the numbers, use a comma to separate them, or rewrite the sentence:

> The show consisted of 3 one-act plays.
> There are 35 thirty-nine-cent stamps left on this roll.
> In 1982, sixteen incumbent senators were defeated.
> There were 16 incumbent senators defeated in 1982.

Specific amounts of money are written in figures. The dollar sign is placed before the figure, and the decimal point and zeroes are usually omitted for even dollar amounts:

> $10.90
> $357,928
> $35
> $5 a pair

Remember that indefinite numbers are spelled out; it is only in such cases that *dollar(s)* is used after the number (rather than the dollar sign before):

> He spent about twenty dollars at the market.
> It is estimated to be a forty- to fifty-dollar repair job.

Sums under a dollar are usually expressed in figures, but they may be spelled out in formal writing:

> 35 cents   thirty-five cents

Remember, however, that consistency would demand:

> One item costs $1.25 and the other is $.69.

In legal documents, sums are given in both words and figures:

> The collection of baseball cards has been appraised at five hundred dollars ($500).
> The necklace was appraised at two million dollars ($2 million).

Fractions standing alone are spelled out. If they are used as adjectives, they are usually hyphenated; if they are used as nouns, they may be either open or hyphenated:

> The court awarded them a two-thirds share of the profits.
> She bought one third [*or* one-third] of a pound of basmati rice.

Fractions in mixed numbers are usually expressed in figures; a diagonal line separates the parts of the fraction:

> $3\,^1/_2$
> $20\,^7/_8$
> $9\,^2/_3$

When writing dates in which the day precedes the month, the date should be expressed in spelled-out ordinal numbers:

> I met with her on the sixth of May.
> We will see them again on the twelfth of July.

When the date follows the month, figures are used:

> They are arriving on August 21.
> She was born on January 14, 1950.

In formal writing, numbers applying to years, decades, and centuries are spelled out:

> Nineteen hundred eighty-three was a banner year.
> He often reminisced about what it was like growing up in the sixties.
> Putting an astronaut on the moon before the end of the twentieth century was a goal of the Kennedy administration.

In informal writing, figures are often used. If the date is abbreviated, an apostrophe is used to show the part that has been left out:

> Bill Clinton was elected President in 1992.
> The popularity of this novel remains as strong today as when it was first published in the 1920s.
> I haven't seen him since '73.

Street names above ten are expressed in ordinal figures (in this case two numbers can be placed next to one another):

> My address is 60 31st Street.

You do not need to use *st*, *nd*, *rd*, or *th* if a numbered street is preceded by either *East* or *West*:

> Her office is at 105 West 12 Street.

In formal writing, the time of day is spelled out and, if a whole hour, is used with *o'clock*:

> Orders will be taken beginning at ten o'clock.
> She arrived at the theater at quarter to eight.

For exact time, figures are used with AM and PM and occasionally with *o'clock*. Whole hours include zeroes:

> The wedding reception will be held from 11:00 AM to 2:30 PM.
> Business hours are from 9:30 AM to 5:00 PM.

Figures are used to express exact dimensions, sizes, measurements, and temperatures:

> The painting measures 2 by 4 feet.

(In technical writing, *x* is used to indicate *by* and " and ' to indicate *inches* and *feet,* respectively.)

> A mile equals 1,760 yards or 5,280 feet.
> At birth the baby weighed 6 pounds 7 ounces.
> The high today was 82°F.

Percentages in text are expressed in figures and are most often followed by the word *percent*:

> All plan members received a 10 percent discount.

Numbers that appear with abbreviations or symbols are written as figures regardless of the size of the number:

> 3%   32°F   5 mm

Grammar is a system of basic rules by which the words in a language are structured and arranged in sentences. It is a system that can be a challenge to understand, in part because the term itself can be used in more than one way.

At its most fundamental, grammar refers to the system of rules that allows speakers of a language to create sentences. Its rules govern word order, the formation of words, and the use of inflections, such as *–s*, to make plurals or *–ed* to form the past tense. This type of grammar is unconsciously learned by nearly every child who has heard a particular language spoken since birth.

Grammar is also used to refer to a set of rules that establish a standard for usage and govern what is sometimes called "good" or "correct" grammar, especially in written communication. This kind of grammar must be consciously taught, even to native speakers of a language, and can be hard to remember. The following section deals with the often difficult-to-remember rules that are included in the grammar of the English language.

Parts of speech

Traditionally, words are classified by the ways in which they function in a sentence. These classifications are called *parts of speech*. Knowing what parts of speech do will help you understand how words are used in sentences. This in turn will help you to avoid making mistakes in sentence construction. The parts of speech that are described here are the noun, pronoun, verb, adjective, adverb, preposition, and conjunction.

Nouns

A *noun* is a word that names a person (*Joe, editor*), place (*Dallas, town*), thing (*book*), or abstraction (*faithfulness*). Nouns can be either *proper* or *common*. Proper nouns name specific persons, places, or things (*Joe, Dallas, Internet*) and are usually capitalized. Common nouns are sometimes classified as *abstract nouns,* which name ideas, beliefs, or qualities (*freedom, biology, capitalism*), or *concrete nouns,* which name tangible things (*chair, computer*).

A noun can function in a sentence in a number of ways. It can serve as the subject of a sentence or a clause:

> The *children* are playing outside.

It can function as the *direct object* of a verb:

> The teacher watched the *children*.

It can be the *object* of a preposition:

> The photographer took a picture of the *children*.

It can serve as the *indirect object* of a verb:

> We gave the *children* a new ball.

As these examples show, the form of the noun is the same regardless of its function.

Most nouns form their plurals by adding –*s*, or in some cases, –*es*, to the singular form (*frogs, potatoes, telephones*). These are called *regular plurals*. Other nouns have *irregular plurals*, indicated by a change in the base form or vowel (*mouse, mice*). A few words, such as *ox* and *child*, have plurals that end in –*en* (*oxen, children*). Some nouns have more than one acceptable plural form (*phenomena, phenomenons*) while others undergo no change to indicate number (*deer, sheep*). Finally, certain nouns may be used as both singular and plural nouns (*physics, politics*), depending on what meaning is intended.

Regardless of whether the plural is regular or irregular, though, a plural noun takes the plural form of a verb:

> The boys hit the girls.
> The oxen pull the wagon.
> The phenomena have yet to be explained.

Collective nouns are nouns that refer to a collection of persons or things that is regarded as a unit (*committee, jury, flock, congress*). Such a noun takes a singular verb when it refers to the collection as a whole and a plural verb when it refers to the members of the collection as separate persons or things:

> The *committee was* in executive session.
> The *committee have* all left for the day.
> The *jury is* sequestered in the hotel.

Pronouns that refer to collective nouns used must agree in number with the noun:

> The *company is* determined to press *its* [not *their*] claim.
> The *jury are* fighting about their verdict.

Possessive forms of a noun are generally formed by adding *'s* to the singular and an apostrophe (') to plural nouns that end in *–s:*

> The *dog's* toys were strewn about the yard.
> The *girl's* clothes are packed in this suitcase.
> The *man's* suit is made of wool flannel.

If the plural is irregular and does not end in *–s,* then *'s* is added to the plural form:

> The *dogs'* toys were strewn about the yard.
> The *girls'* clothes are packed in these suitcases.
> The *men's* suits are made of wool flannel.

The same possessive forms are used when the possessives are in the predicate:

> These are the *dog's*.   These are the *dogs'*.

Pronouns

A pronoun is a word that functions as a substitute for a noun. A pronoun refers to a person or thing that has been named or understood in a particular context. There are several kinds of pronouns, and one pronoun may serve a variety of functions.

Personal pronouns have different forms for first, second, and third person. *I* and *we* are first-person pronouns, *you* is the second-person pronoun, and *he, she, it, we,* and *they* are third-person pronouns:

> *We* will produce the program, and *they* will distribute it.
> *I* am glad that *she* was willing to help.

Relative pronouns introduce a dependent clause. The pronouns *who, that,* and *which* are relative pronouns. *Who* is used with persons; *that* is used with persons, animals, or inanimate objects; and *which* is used with animals or inanimate objects:

She is a leader *who* is destined for greatness.
The house *that* has green shutters is for sale.
The new restaurant, *which* opened yesterday, features Italian food.

Interrogative pronouns, such as *who*, *which*, and *what*, introduce a direct question:

What do you want us to do?
Which of these sweaters are you going to wear?

Demonstrative pronouns, such as *this*, *that*, *these*, and *those*, refer to specific persons or things:

That is the latest policy directive.
This is the best book I have read in years.

Indefinite pronouns refer to persons and things that are not specified or identified. Some examples are *all*, *any*, *anybody*, *anyone*, *anything*, *each*, *either*, *everybody*, *everything*, *few*, *neither*, *nobody*, *none*, *one*, *several*, and *some*:

Anybody with any luck can win at this game.
We brought *everything* except the silverware.
Some will no doubt drop out at the last minute.

Reflexive pronouns end in –*self* or –*selves* and are used as the direct or indirect object of a verb or as the object of a preposition:

He bought *himself* a new computer.
We treated *ourselves* to an ice cream.

Reflexive pronouns usually refer to the subject of the sentence. They can also be used as an appositive to a noun or pronoun for emphasis:

I *myself* prefer a less crowded office.
The book was signed by the author *herself*.

Pronouns can be further classified by grammatical *case* (nominative, possessive, or objective), *number* (singular or plural), *person* (first, second, or third), and *gender* (masculine, feminine, or neuter).

The *case* of a pronoun is determined by its function in the sentence. The *nominative case*, which includes the pronouns *I*, *we*, *you*, *he*, *she*, *it*, *they*, and *who*, is required when the pronoun is the subject of a sentence or clause:

We are ready to go.

Tennis is a sport that *he* plays very well.

A traditional grammatical rule also requires that the nominative case be used after forms of the verb *be*:

This is *he*.   It is *I*.

These constructions can sound pompous and stilted, however, and should probably be avoided.

Another grammatical rule requires the nominative case in formal writing after the conjunctions *as* and *than*:

She is a faster skater than *I*.   She skates as fast as *he*.

These constructions can sound needlessly formal, unless you include a verb to follow the pronoun:

She skates as fast as *he* does.

We are even more upset than *they* are.

The *possessive case* includes the pronouns *my, mine, our, ours, your, yours, his, her, hers, its, their, theirs,* and *whose*. This case is required to show relationships such as possession and origin:

Our house was just painted.

Their work is outstanding.

His paintings are on display in the museum.

A traditional grammatical rule also requires the possessive case before a gerund:

Susan could understand *his* [not *him*] wanting to go.

The *objective case* includes the pronouns *me, us, you, him, her, it, them,* and *whom*. This case is required when the pronoun serves any of several functions in the sentence:

The object of a verb:

The good news delighted *him*.

The fall in sales disturbs *us*.

The object of a participle or gerund:

He spoke rapidly, urging *her* to be on time.

Meeting *him* was an interesting experience.

The object of a preposition:

Between *you* and *me*, the new policy won't work.

The object of a verb that has been omitted from a clause following *as* or *than*:

> He likes Melissa more than [he likes] *me*.
> The boss praised Anne as much as [she praised] *them*.

An appositive to a noun that is an object:

> The company promoted two sales representatives—Jennifer Black and *me*—last week.

Pronouns used as subjects should agree with their verbs in *number*; that is, singular pronouns take singular verbs and plural pronouns take plural verbs:

> *He has* a good job.
> *They have* good jobs.

Problems in number agreement are often caused by indefinite pronouns such as *anyone* and *everybody*. It is often difficult to know which pronoun to choose in sentences such as this one:

> Everyone thinks (*he is/she is/they are*) entitled to a raise.

This problem also occurs in sentences with personal pronouns that refer to nouns of indefinite gender:

> A good judge must never indulge (*his/her/their*) personal prejudices.

The traditional solution has been to use *he*, *him*, and *his* in these cases to stand as the representative member of the group being discussed. But this usage has been attacked as sexist. To avoid gender bias, many people sometimes use compound pronouns such as *his or her*. These constructions can be cumbersome when used on a sustained basis, however. Other people choose to override the standard grammatical rule of number agreement and use *their* to refer to a singular noun of indefinite gender:

> Everyone must take their assignment home.

Perhaps the best solution to this problem is to write in the plural:

> All students must take their assignments home.

Personal pronouns are classified as *first*, *second*, or *third person*, and must agree with their verbs accordingly. *First person* refers to the speaker or speakers:

> *I* am happy.   *We* are not worried.

Second person refers to the person or persons being addressed:

> *You* will never change.

Third person refers to the person or thing being talked about:

> *He* looks like his grandmother.
> *She* is very wealthy.
> *It* is a very big sandwich.
> *They* are buying a house.

When using any type of pronoun, it is important that you construct the sentence so that your reader clearly understands which noun the pronoun refers to. Unclear antecedents occur when more than one noun can logically be the antecedent to any given pronoun:

> Marie told Lucy that she had won the prize.

In this example, it is unclear whether *she* refers to Marie or Lucy. Technically, a pronoun is supposed to refer to the nearest antecedent, but this rule is not always strictly followed. Sentences containing unclear antecedents cannot be corrected by a simple repositioning of words; they must be rewritten:

> Marie had won the prize, and she told Lucy about it.
> Lucy had won the prize, and Marie told her about it.

Verbs

A *verb* is a word that expresses action (*jump*, *open*, *speak*) or a state of being (*is*, *exist*). Verbs are usually classified as *main* or *auxiliary*, *transitive* or *intransitive*, and *regular* or *irregular*.

Most verbs are *main* verbs. Main verbs change their form by adding suffixes to agree with their subject, such as *he goes* or *she runs*, and to form participles, such as *sleeping* and *slept*. Main verbs also follow *not* and require a form of the verb *do* to form the negatives:

I do not *enjoy* bowling.

In questions main verbs must use a form of *do* and always follow the subject:

Do you *live* in this building?

Main verbs also take an infinitive with *to*:

I *promised* to call him tonight.

Auxiliary verbs are sometimes called *helping* verbs because they help complete the form and meaning of main verbs. There are several features that distinguish auxiliary verbs:

Auxiliary verbs do not take word endings to form participles or to agree in number with their subject:

She *may* [not *mays*] go to the store.

Auxiliary verbs come before *not* and do not use *do* to form the negative:

You *might* not like that.

Auxiliary verbs come before the subject in a question and do not use *do*:

Would you like to go to the movies?

Auxiliary verbs take the infinitive without *to*:

I *will* call you tomorrow.

A *transitive* verb is a verb that has an object:

She *worked* the keyboard with nimble fingers.

An *intransitive* verb is a verb that does not have an object:

She *worked* hard.

Regular verbs form the past tense and the past participle by adding *–d* or *–ed* to the base form:

He *called* this morning.

Irregular verbs do not follow the *–ed* pattern of regular verbs. Irregular verbs form the past tense and the past participle by changing their base form, often by changing their vowel:

He *did* the work.   He *has done* the work.

Examples of irregular verbs include the verbs *begin* (*begin*, *began*, *begun*), *draw* (*draw*, *drew*, *drawn*), *meet* (*meet*, *met*, *met*), *stand* (*stand*, *stood*, *stood*), and *think* (*think*, *thought*, *thought*).

Transitive verbs have a property, known as *voice*, that can express the relation between the subject and the verb in one of two ways. Verbs in the *active* voice have the performer of the action as the subject:

Linda *found* the ring.   Bob *signed* the contract.

In the *passive* voice, the situation is reversed. The person or thing that is acted upon becomes the subject, and the performer of the action is put in a phrase beginning with *by* or is left out of the sentence:

The ring *was found* by Linda.   The contract *was signed*.

Passive verb phrases consist of a form of the verb *be* and a past participle. Passive verbs may occur in any tense and may use an auxiliary verb:

The contract *has been signed*.   The ring *may have been lost*.

As the name implies, the passive voice tends to be weaker than the active voice. Passive verbs also require more words than their active counterparts. For these reasons, writers often avoid the passive unless they do not want to be direct.

A *mood* is a set of verb forms that convey the attitude of the speaker about the likelihood or factuality of what is said. English has three moods: *indicative*, *subjunctive*, and *imperative*:

The indicative mood of a verb states a fact or asks a question:

You *know* the procedure.   *Does* he ever get up early?

The *subjunctive* mood of a verb expresses wishes, commands, or conditions that are contrary to fact. The subjunctive is usually used after a conjunction such as *if*, *though*, *lest*, *that*, *till*, or *unless*:

If I *were* you, I would recommend a change in that policy.

For most verbs the subjunctive is identical to the base form of the verb, and is only noticeable in the third person:

I insist that the chairman *resign*!

Note that *resign* does not end in –*s* to agree in number with *chairman*, as it would if it were in the indicative mood.

In general, the subjunctive has limited use in English, its functions largely being performed by auxiliary verbs like *might*, *should*, and *would*.

The imperative mood of a verb expresses a request or command, often with the subject omitted:

Hand me the new manual, please.

The *tense* of a verb specifies the time or nature of the action that occurs and is designated as past, present, or future:

I *walked* to work this morning.
I *enjoy* walking to work.
I *will walk* to work tomorrow.

When past, present, or future action is described as completed, or *perfected*, it is in the *past perfect*, *present perfect*, or *future perfect* tense:

I *had walked* to work by the time you got up.
I *have walked* to work.
I *will have walked* to work by the time you get up.

When past, present, or future action is expressed as being in progress, or *progressive*, it is in the *past progressive*, *present progressive*, or *future progressive* tense:

I *was walking* to work yesterday when the thunderstorm began.
I *am walking* to work this morning.
I *will be walking* to work until my car is repaired.

A verb must agree with its subject in *person* (first, second, third) and *number* (singular, plural), as described in the following table. For example, a first-person singular verb is used with the simple subject *I*, and a third-person singular verb is used with any singular noun or third-person singular pronoun.

	Singular	*Plural*
first person	I send	we send
second person	you send	you send
third person	he/she/it sends	they send

It can be difficult to apply this rule. Here are some special cases of the rule:

The conjunction *and* joins two simple subjects in a compound plural subject and demands a plural verb:

> John and Jane *walk* out on the boardwalk. (third-person plural verb)
> Jane and I *walk* out on the boardwalk. (first-person plural verb)

The conjunction *or* does not form a plural subject from two singular nouns or pronouns and therefore takes a singular rather than a plural verb:

> Either John or Jane *gets* a paper each day. (third-person singular verb)

In addition, certain words and expressions sometimes pose problems in connection with *subject-verb agreement*. For example, a verb must agree with the subject even when a singular or plural prepositional phrase intervenes:

> A deck of cards *sits* on the shelf. (third-person singular verb, subject is *deck*, *cards* is the object of the preposition *of*)

A verb must agree with its singular subject, not with a plural phrase that follows the verb:

> The *topic* of my memo *is* the many different types of procedural errors that have occurred during this trial.

A verb must agree with its subject even when expressions intervene:

> The *executive*, along with a receptionist and two secretaries, *is* in charge of registrations.

A verb having a singular subject preceded by *each*, *every*, *many a*, *such a*, or *no* must be singular in number even when two or more of such subjects are linked by *and*:

> *Each* manager and *each* division chief *has urged* the employees to invest in the thrift plan.

A verb should agree with the subject closest to it when *either-or* and *neither-nor* are used:

Neither the supervisor nor the union *members are* willing to negotiate.

Participles are *verbal adjectives.* Although the present participle of a regular verb is also formed by adding *–ing,* it is used as an adjective modifying a noun rather than as a noun:

He shouted over the *roaring* engine.

Past participles are also used in this way:

He fixed the *broken vase.*
Tired workers tend to make mistakes.

Adjectives

Adjectives modify words, phrases, and clauses that serve as nouns and pronouns. An adjective describes, qualifies, limits, or otherwise makes a word distinct and separate from something else:

a *tall* building   a *reasonable* offer
a *beautiful* garden

Adjectives may occur in the *positive, comparative,* or *superlative* degree. The regular forms of comparison are made by adding *–er* (comparative) or *–est* (superlative) to the positive form of the adjective:

the *easy* method   the *easier* method
the *easiest* method

Most adjectives with two or more syllables require *more* or *most,* rather than *–er* or *–est,* to form the comparative and superlative:

the *reliable* source   the *more reliable* source
the *most reliable* source

Irregular adjectives have comparative and superlative forms that are not derived from the positive, or uncompared, form of the adjective:

a *good* suggestion   a *better* suggestion
the *best* suggestion

Adjectives can also be compared in a decreasing way using *less* and *least,* as in *less skillful* and *least skillful.* Some adjectives (*asleep*, *nonexistent*) cannot be compared. Many technical terms (*biological*, *hydrodynamic*, *linguistic*) fall into this category.

Adverbs

An *adverb* may modify a verb (She reads *fast*), an adjective (She is a *very* fast reader), or another adverb (She can read *very* fast). There are several types of adverbs. For example, a *sentence* adverb modifies an entire clause or sentence:

> *Unfortunately*, the advertisement did not get the desired results.

An *interrogative* adverb is used in asking or stating a direct or indirect question:

> *How* are you feeling?   *Where* did you go?

A *conjunctive* adverb connects sentences:

> The conference is over; *however*, there is still work to be done.

Some adverbs can be identified by determining whether they express time (*already*, *finally*, *lately*, *never*, *now*, *then*), place (*above*, *far*, *here*, *near*, *there*, *upstairs*), manner (*easily*, *otherwise*, *surely*, *well*), degree (*equally*, *fully*, *less*, *much*, *too*), cause or purpose (*consequently*, *therefore*, *wherefore*, *why*), or number (*first/firstly*, *second/secondly*, *third/thirdly*).

Like adjectives, regular and irregular adverbs can be compared by using the *comparative* or *superlative* form of the *positive* adverb. Regular adverbs commonly add the words *more* and *most* or *less* and *least* to form the comparative or superlative forms of the adverb, although a few can add the word endings *–er* (*sooner*) and *–est* (*soonest*):

> He is *often* available on Fridays.
> He is *more often* available on Fridays.
> He is *most often* available on Fridays.

Also like adjectives, some adverbs use different forms to indicate comparison rather than adding a word ending such as *–er* or requiring a word such as *more*:

> He did *badly* on the test.
> He did *worse* on the test than she did.
> Of all the students in the class, he did *worst* on the test.

Prepositions

A preposition connects and shows the relationship between a noun or pronoun and other words in a sentence. The noun or pronoun is the *object* of the preposition. The preposition together with the noun or pronoun is a *prepositional phrase*:

> in the room
> out of paper
> under the desk

Prepositional phrases can indicate a variety of situations or conditions including the following:

> Joe attended the meeting *with several colleagues.* (accompaniment)
> The trip was canceled *because of bad weather.* (cause)
> Those who are not *for us* are *against us.* (support or opposition)
> We drove *to the city.* (destination)
> I have everything *but a private office.* (exception)
> The arrogance *of that official* defies description. (possession)
> I want a desk *of polished mahogany.* (composition or makeup)
> I worked out the problem *with my personal computer.* (means or instrument)
> Treat all visitors *with courtesy.* (manner)
> I ran *across the hall* to find you. (direction)
> John is *in the study.* (location)
> They'll do anything *for a quick profit.* (purpose or intention)
> The new manager is *from Chicago.* (origin)
> Call me *at noon.* (time)

Many familiar words that are used as prepositions, such as *in*, *to*, and *off*, can also function as other parts of speech, particularly as adverbs. *Above*, for example, can be used as an adverb (The balloon floated *above*), adjective (The *above* figures are correct), and noun (Read the *above* for information about verbs) as well as a preposition.

Conjunctions

A *conjunction* links words, phrases, clauses, or sentences and is used to show how one element is related to another. The three principal types of conjunctions are *coordinate*, *subordinate*, and *correlative.* Conjunctive adverbs, such as *besides, however,* and *nevertheless,* also connect sentences and words.

Coordinate conjunctions, such as *and, but, for, or, nor,* and *yet,* connect elements of equal value:

> He is the president of the company, *and* he is our boss.
> She is successful *but* modest.
> Jim had to act as coach, *for* Bill was sick.

Subordinate conjunctions, such as *as if, because, in case, inasmuch as, provided that, since, when,* and *where,* connect a subordinate element to another element in a sentence:

> *Because* the report is late, the meeting will have to be postponed.
> Andrew is a skilled writer, *although* he has difficulty researching complex subjects.

Correlative conjunctions, such as *as . . . so, both . . . and, either . . . or, not only . . . but also,* and *whether . . . or,* are used in pairs or a series. Correlatives connect elements of equal value and must be positioned correctly in the sentence to avoid confusion:

> Overpopulation has been a problem *both* in India *and* in China.
> We are having pot roast, *whether* you like it *or* not.
> *Either* the executive *or* the assistant is coming.

Subject and predicate

A *sentence* is an independent grammatical unit that has at least one *subject* and one *predicate*. In some sentences, such as imperative sentences, the subject is understood. The simplest standard sentence has a noun or pronoun that serves as the subject of the sentence (underlined in the following examples) and a verb (italicized in the following examples):

<u>I</u> *sleep.*   <u>Kittens</u> *play.*
<u>He</u> *eats.*   <u>You</u> *fell.*

A written sentence ends in a period, question mark, or exclamation point. There are various types of sentences, including those discussed later in *Sentence Functions,* beginning on page 70.

The predicate of a sentence consists of the verb and any words that are governed by or that modify the verb, and it tells what action the subject is performing or what action is being performed on the subject. The simplest predicate possible consists of only a verb:

The clown *danced.*

A simple subject-and-verb sentence has an *intransitive* verb, one that does not require or cannot take an object:

The cat *purred.*
The bell *rang.*

Direct object

If the verb takes a *direct object*, it is called a *transitive* verb. The direct object is part of the predicate of a sentence.

The basic sentence pattern for a transitive verb consists of a subject, verb, and direct object (italicized in these examples):

I like *you.*   We played *checkers.*
He eats *strawberries.*   Henry outran *Charlie.*

Notice that in most cases the word order indicates which is the subject and which is the direct object. The form of the word does not change; only its position changes. In the following examples the direct object is highlighted in italics, the verb is underlined, and the subject is unmarked:

> Henry <u>hit</u> *the ball.*
> The ball <u>hit</u> *Henry.*
>
> Lisa <u>likes</u> *someone.*
> Someone <u>likes</u> *Lisa.*

Sentences can be lengthened by modifying the subject, the predicate, or both. These modifications usually add information to the sentences. Each detail makes a sentence more specific.

Modifying the subject

The subject of a sentence is usually modified by adding articles, demonstrative adjectives (such as *this* or *that*), adjectives, and noun-modifiers. Adjectives can themselves be modified by *adverbs*.

Notice the ways details can be given to the subject of the simple sentence "The cat eats fish":

> The *striped* cat eats fish.
> The *striped tawny* cat eats fish.
> *My striped tawny* cat eats fish.
> *That pathetically skinny alley* cat eats fish.

Modifying the predicate

In the predicate of a sentence, the verb or one of its objects may be modified. Articles, pronouns, and adjectives may modify the direct object. Adverbs may modify the verb itself. Adverbs or adverbial phrases may also modify the adjectives that modify direct objects. Below, the simple sentence "The dog jumps fences" is made more specific as details are added to the predicate:

> The dog jumps *picket* fences.
> The dog jumps *our neighbor's picket* fence.
> The dog jumps *that* fence *quickly.*
> The dog jumps *our neighbor's freshly painted picket* fence *quickly.*

Notice the different functions of the adverbs, *freshly* and *quickly.* The adverb *freshly* modifies *painted*—an adjective. The adverb *quickly* modifies *jump*—the verb.

Indirect object

An *indirect object* is a noun or pronoun that identifies the person *to whom* or *for whom* an action is performed or the thing *to which* or *for which* an action is done. The indirect object follows a verb in the active voice and precedes the direct object. The best way to identify an indirect object is to imagine that the word *to* or *for* precedes it as you read the sentence. The following examples show the indirect object in italics and the direct object underlined:

> Tom gave *Jenny* a gift.
> He told *Sarah* the news.
> They built *themselves* a house.
> Ellen cooked *the family* a meal.

If, however, the word *to* or *for* is actually part of the sentence, the noun or pronoun that follows it will be the object of the preposition *to* or *for*, rather than an indirect object. The examples above can be rewritten to make the indirect object in each the object of a *prepositional phrase*. In the following examples the direct object is underlined and the prepositional phrase is in italics:

> Tom gave a gift *to Jenny*.
> They built a house *for themselves*.
> He told the news *to Sarah*.
> Ellen cooked a meal *for the family*.

Be and other linking verbs

A few verbs take as complements nouns or adjectives that refer to the subject. These verbs are called *linking verbs* and form the predicate by linking the subject to a noun or adjective. The most common linking verb is the verb *be* and all its forms. Certain other verbs such as *appear, seem, look, taste,* or *smell* may follow the same pattern when they function as linking verbs.

The important point to note is that the adjective that occurs in the predicate part of the sentence modifies the subject. Such adjectives are known as *predicate adjectives* or *predicate complements*. The following examples show the predicate adjectives in italics:

Joan is *clever*.   The mouse seems *frightened*.
John appears *tall*.   The soup tastes *delicious*.

Sometimes the verb *be* links two nouns. In these cases, the noun that follows *be* is not an object. It is known as a *predicate nominative*. The following examples show the predicate nominative in italics:

I am *a person.*   The sign had been *a beacon.*
Eddie was *a tenor.*   They were *the leaders.*

There used to begin a sentence

Sentences can begin with the adverb *there*:

There are ten people in the room.
There is hope.
There does not seem to be any chance.
There may be some left.

In such sentences, *there* is not the subject. In fact, when *there* begins a sentence, it usually signals that the verb comes before the subject. Thus the verb must agree with the noun or pronoun that follows it, especially in sentences containing a verb such as *be*, *seem*, or *appear*. In the following examples, the subject has been underlined:

There is a great <u>deli</u> across the street.
In this direction, though, *there* seem to be <u>trees</u> obscuring the view.

Passive voice sentences

All the sentences discussed so far have been in the *active voice*. In the active voice, the subject performs the action expressed by the verb, and the direct object, when there is one, receives the action.

In the *passive voice*, the subject receives the action of the verb. Passive constructions are formed by making the direct object of a transitive verb into the grammatical subject of a passive verb. The first two examples below are sentences in the active voice. They are rewritten in the passive voice for the following two examples. Notice that the verb (underlined) agrees with the subject (italicized). Notice also that a form of the verb *be* (underlined and italicized) is needed to form the passive:

Amy <u>found</u> the treasure.   *The treasure* <u>*was* found</u> by Amy.
Paul <u>hears</u> the bells.   *The bells* <u>*are* heard</u> by Paul.

The use of the passive voice places the emphasis on the receiver of the action. This kind of emphasis is important in many kinds of writing. It is useful when the persons or things performing the action are unknown, unimportant, or unidentified. For instance, it is important in news reporting when sources may not be named. The passive voice is also found in scientific and technical writing, where it is often the preferred style. In general, you can use the passive voice to focus attention on the object of the verb's action.

Although many composition books warn against excessive use of the passive, you need not avoid it completely—just use it wisely. Even in writing about movement, the passive has its place:

> Slugger *was hit* by the pitch.

The writer could have written the sentence in the active voice:

> The pitch *hit* Slugger.

But this construction would place the emphasis on *the pitch* instead of *Slugger* and would change the intended meaning of the sentence.

Coordinate elements

Most of the sentences examined so far have been fairly simple in structure. In each example there is generally only one subject, one verb, and one of each kind of object, so it is fairly easy to identify these parts of the sentence.

Sentences can, however, grow far more complex. A sentence may have several subjects, verbs, or objects; it may have many phrases and clauses. The more complicated a sentence becomes, the more difficult it may be to identify the subject and predicate.

One of the simplest ways to enlarge a simple sentence is to use more than one subject, verb, or object. When there are multiple elements, it is important to keep them parallel in form. The multiple elements may be subjects:

> *Dogs and cats* run wild in the street.
> *Men and women* played tennis.
> *Wisdom and learning* are not the same.
> *Sheep, horses, and pigs* live on the farm.

Avoid ill-matched combinations, such as "Wisdom, learning, and to know are not the same." "To know" is an infinitive and does not fit the same pattern established by "Wisdom, learning . . . " "Wisdom, learning, and knowledge . . ." would be better.

The multiple subject may be a series of phrases instead of individual words:

> *Going to school, keeping house, and maintaining a job* complicate her life.
> *Antique tapestries from France, handwoven Navaho blankets, and Early American samplers* cover the walls.

There should be no comma between the last subject and the verb. And, of course, the verb must agree with the subject.

It is acceptable either to repeat the preposition or to allow one preposition to govern the various elements: "Dreams *of* wealth, (*of*) fame, and (*of*) happiness kept her going." (When *of* appears only once, "Wealth, fame, and happiness" are all understood to be objects of the preposition *of*.) Good style would be to use the preposition once and allow it to work for all applicable elements or to repeat it with each element. Avoid a mixture: "Dreams *of* wealth, fame, and *of* happiness kept her going."

The same preposition may not work for all the elements in a series. It is then necessary to give the appropriate preposition for each element.

The multiple elements may also be verbs:

> He *cut, fit, and sewed* the clothes in one day.
> She *tried, failed, and tried* again.
> The children *dried* their tears *and began* to sing.

Note that two or more verbs may accompany a single subject. Sometimes the verbs are simple. Sometimes, as in the third example, there may be more than one predicate.

In these cases, each verb may have its own objects or modifiers. A comma should not separate the subject from either verb:

> We *ate* our sandwiches and *drank* our milk.
> Jimmy *waved* good-bye to his friends and *drove* home slowly.

When using auxiliary and main verbs, it is important to make sure that the tenses are consistent. It is easy to forget that the auxiliary verb governs all the verbs in the series. In the example "He has *come* and *gone*," the verb *gone* is correct. *Went* would not be correct because the auxiliary verb *has* governs both past participles.

In the example "The time machine *has not been*, and perhaps never *will be*, invented," two different auxiliary verbs are needed. *Has been* establishes the present perfect tense and *will be* serves for the future. The past participle *invented* works with both auxiliaries.

The multiple elements in a coordinate construction may be objects—either direct objects, as in the first three examples, or indirect objects, as in the final two examples:

> We ate *fish* and *chips*.
> Felicia bought *books*, *clothes*, and *CDs*.
> I enjoy *going to movies*, *riding a motorcycle*, and *building birdhouses*.
> Give *Tom*, *Dick*, and *Lyle* the tickets.
> Did you throw *him* or *her* the ball?

In each example given thus far there has been one subject and multiple verbs, multiple subjects and one verb, or one subject and verb and several objects. There may also be multiple verbs, subjects, and objects in one sentence:

> Dick and Jane walked or ran all the way. (two subjects, two verbs)
> The cat and the kitten sniffed and ate the fish and chicken. (two subjects, two verbs, two direct objects)
> The cat and the kitten ate the fish and drank the milk. (two subjects, two verbs, two direct objects; both subjects govern both verbs but each verb has its own direct object)

Clauses

A *clause* is a group of words that has a subject and a predicate. A clause may be *independent* or *subordinate*.

An independent clause can be a sentence in itself. It can also be the main clause of a larger sentence. The main clause is sometimes called the basic sentence.

A subordinate clause also has a subject and a predicate, but it cannot stand by itself as a complete sentence. It depends on the main clause. The subordinate clause is sometimes called a dependent clause:

> If it rains, we'll go home.

We'll go home can stand as a separate sentence. It is an independent clause. *If it rains,* on the other hand, cannot stand alone as a sentence. It is a subordinate clause.

Compound sentences

Two or more independent clauses can be connected to make a *compound sentence.* There are several ways to join the independent clauses of compound sentences. A comma and a *coordinate conjunction* such as *and, and so, but, or, nor, for, yet,* or *so* may be used:

> I tried to buy sugar, but the store was out of it.
> He will pick up the package tomorrow, or you will have to mail it.
> Henry will prepare the dessert, Molly will make the salad, and I'll cook the main course.

Notice that the last example has more than two independent clauses. In a series of three or more independent clauses, use a comma alone between all but the last two clauses.

A semicolon may be used if there is no coordinate conjunction:

> John didn't win the match; he didn't even try.

A comma may be used instead of a semicolon, but only in very short sentences:

> Sometimes you win, sometimes you lose.

A coordinate conjunction alone may be used, especially if the two clauses are very short:

> We tried and we failed.

Each of the above examples can be rewritten as two or more separate sentences:

> I tried to buy sugar. The store was out of it.
> He will pick up the package tomorrow. You will have to mail it.
> Henry will prepare the dessert. Molly will make the salad. I'll cook the main course.
> John didn't win the match. He didn't even try.
> Sometimes you win. Sometimes you lose.
> We tried. We failed.

The subjects of the independent clauses in a sentence may be identical, or they may be different. But the subject must be stated in each clause. If it is not, the sentence is not a compound sentence:

> He ran, and he jumped.
> He ran and jumped.

The first sentence is a compound sentence because it can be separated into two sentences: "He ran. He jumped." The second sentence is not a compound sentence because its subject is stated only once. It is a simple sentence with a compound predicate.

It is important to recognize the difference between these two kinds of sentences so you can punctuate them correctly. The first sentence should have a comma before *and*, but the second should not.

Because independent clauses can be combined into a single sentence, some writers have a tendency to overdo the combining or to use incorrect punctuation. Some common errors that arise from this tendency are *run-on sentences*, *comma splices*, and *fused sentences*.

Run-on sentences. Sentences in which too many independent clauses have been combined are called *run-on sentences*. They are difficult to read. Run-on sentences can usually be corrected by separating the clauses into individual sentences. The conjunctions that connect the clauses of a run-on sentence can then be eliminated. The following example is a run-on sentence; the second example is its corrected version:

> The wicked witch cast a spell *so* the prince fell asleep, *and* the princess didn't know what to do, *but* the queen sent the knight to fight the dragon, *then* the prince awoke.

> The wicked witch cast a spell. The prince fell asleep, and the princess didn't know what to do. The queen sent the knight to fight the dragon. Then the prince awoke.

Comma splices. A *comma splice* occurs when a comma separates the main clauses of a compound sentence:

> The moon hid behind a cloud, all the world turned dark.

This type of writing error can be corrected in one of four ways. You can correct it by inserting a coordinating conjunction:

The moon hid behind a cloud, *and* all the world turned dark.

You can correct it by replacing the comma with a semicolon:

The moon hid behind a cloud; all the world turned dark.

You can correct it by rewriting the clauses to make separate sentences:

The moon hid behind a cloud. All the world turned dark.

You can correct it by turning one clause into a subordinate clause:

When the moon hid behind a cloud, all the world turned dark.

Fused sentences. When two or more sentences are joined without punctuation, they are said to be *fused sentences*:

He didn't ask me he just did it.
John said he was going to enter the big race then his mother said that she would not allow it.

Correct fused sentences by separating them into individual sentences:

He didn't ask me. He just did it.
John said he was going to enter the big race. Then his mother said that she would not allow it.

Complex sentences

A *complex sentence* has one independent clause and at least one subordinate clause. The subordinate clause is introduced by a *subordinate conjunction* such as *if, because, although, when, as soon as, whenever, even though, before, since, unless,* or *until*.

The subordinate clause may come before or after the main clause. When it comes before the main clause, a comma usually separates the clauses. The following examples show the subordinate clauses in italics:

I'll go to the dance *if my mother lets me.*
Because I laughed, the teacher asked me to leave the room.

He will return *as soon as he has train fare*.
Do you know the man *who sat next to you*?
We enjoyed the party *that you gave*.

Compound-complex sentences

Compound-complex sentences are sentences that have two or more independent clauses and at least one subordinate clause. The following examples highlight the subordinate clause in italics; the independent clauses are underlined:

After the war ended, <u>prices continued to rise, and the black market thrived</u>.
<u>Everybody stopped speaking, and the ticking clock was all that could be heard</u> *when the president took the stage*.
<u>The bell rang, the children filed out of the school, and the teachers checked the classrooms</u> *because they wanted to lock them*.

Subordinate clauses as subjects, objects, modifiers

When *subordinate clauses* occur in sentences, they often fill the job of a particular part of speech. The entire clause may serve as a noun, an adjective, or an adverb.

When a subordinate clause fills the role of a noun, it may serve a number of functions in the sentence. It may serve as a *subject*:

How the pyramids were built remains a mystery.
That she is an impostor cannot be proven.

It may function as an *object of a verb*:

The archaeologist discovered *how the pyramids were built*.
Can you prove *that she is an impostor*?

It may serve as an *object of a preposition*:

John learned about *what had been said*.
She will go to *whatever school she chooses*.

It may function as a *predicate nominative*:

The story is *that he disappeared*.
It seems *that he did run away*.

When a subordinate clause, underlined in the following examples, fills the role of an adverb, it can modify a *verb*:

He will *return* <u>as soon as he has train fare</u>.
Sally will *dance* <u>if you ask her</u>.

It can modify an *adjective*:

The movie was *funnier* <u>than I expected</u>.
Simon is as *tall* <u>as I am</u>.

It can modify another *adverb*:

She ran *quickly* <u>as a gazelle might</u>.
He gossiped more *indiscreetly* <u>than I expected</u>.

When a subordinate clause fills the role of an adjective, under-lined in the examples below, it generally modifies a *noun*:

I like the *dress* <u>that you bought</u>.
I find myself on the *street* <u>where you live</u>.
The *man* <u>who is wise</u> avoids trouble.

In summary, clauses are classified by their function in a sentence and not by the part of speech with which they begin. Thus a noun clause functions as a noun in a sentence but does not begin with a noun, an adverbial clause functions as an adverb in a sentence but does not begin with an adverb, and an adjectival clause functions as an adjective in a sentence but does not start out with an adjective.

Periodic sentences

In a *periodic sentence*, the main clause or its predicate is at the end of the sentence and is preceded by two or more clauses or phrases that are often parallel in construction. The periodic sentence can have a very dramatic effect if it is used well and infrequently, so it is important that the main clause justify the lead-up. The following example of a periodic sentence shows a main clause, high-lighted in italics, preceded by subordinate clauses and by phrases:

Working long hours, saving every penny she could, denying herself luxuries, using every resource she had, *she managed to save enough for an education.*

Phrases and verb forms

A *phrase* is a group of words that together have meaning. Broadly speaking, clauses are phrases that have a subject and a verb, but the term *phrase* usually is applied to meaningful groups of words that do not have a subject and verb.

Phrases may be used to modify nouns, adjectives, verbs, and even complete sentences. Phrases may be used in the same way that single words may be used in a sentence.

Apposition. A noun or pronoun may have a noun or a phrase in *apposition*. That is, a noun or phrase (italicized in the following examples) may appear next to the noun or pronoun and extend its meaning:

> We, *the committee*, are responsible for the decision.
> My brother *Seamus* has red hair.
> The book *under the counter* is rare.
> We thanked our teacher, *Ms. Grimby*.

Notice that either the subject or the object may have a word or phrase in apposition. It is the first noun or pronoun—not the one in apposition—that determines the form of the verb (for example, "We, the committee, *are*," not "We, the committee, *is*," and "You, the organizer, *deserve*," not "You, the organizer, *deserves*").

Object complement. Some verbs seem to have two objects. The second object is not really in apposition to the first; it is instead an *object complement*:

> The council elected Jane *president*.
> We appointed Sara *leader*.

An *adjective* can also be an object complement:

> The heat made the plant *brown*.
> Opposition turned the deal *sour*.

Verb forms in noun positions. *Verbals* are words derived from verbs that are used as nouns or adjectives. Infinitives and gerunds are verbal nouns.

The *subject* of a sentence may be the infinitive of a verb:

> *To travel* requires money.
> *To speak* honestly is sometimes difficult.

Even though the infinitive (*to speak*) may take the place of a noun, its verbal nature is maintained. It is modified by an adverb (*honestly*) as a verb would be modified.

The infinitive can also serve as an *object*:

> He likes *to knit*.   He wants *to play* hockey.

The object (*to play*) resembles a verb in that it has its own object (*hockey*), but it also functions as a noun.

A *gerund* is the *–ing* form of a verb that functions as a noun. A gerund may serve as a subject or as an object:

> *Traveling* requires money.
> His *going* relieves us of a problem.
> Good *singing* gives us pleasure.
> *Singing* well gives us pleasure.

Note that a gerund (*singing*) may be modified by an adjective (*good*) or an adverb (*well*). When the gerund has more of a noun sense, an adjective modifies it; when it has more of a verb sense, an adverb modifies it.

Gerunds have more noun functions than infinitives do. Gerunds may be used in apposition, as object complements, and as objects of prepositions, where infinitives may not.

Modifiers. A *modifier* is a word, a phrase, a clause, or a whole sentence that specifies or limits the meaning of a word, a phrase, a clause, or a whole sentence.

Since a clause or a phrase may function as an adjective, an adverb, or a noun, the phrase or clause that acts as a modifier must be placed in the correct relationship to the word it modifies:

> *Having seen the house*, she left.
> *Thinking he would be given a raise*, he went to work.

Although these examples are grammatically acceptable, the sentences could also be rewritten:

> She left *having seen the house*.
> He went to work *thinking he would be given a raise*.

The sentences still make sense because the modifying phrase logically applies to the pronouns (*she* and *he*).

Dangling modifiers. A *dangling modifier* occurs when a modifier does not modify the subject of the main clause. It most often appears at the beginning of a sentence. Sentences that have a dangling modifier must be rewritten. The following sentences contain dangling modifiers, shown in italics:

> *Though sick*, I saw him at work.
> *After running the race*, we saw him faint.

Rewriting can eliminate such modifiers:

> Though he was sick, I saw him at work.
> We saw him faint after running the race.

Notice that the problem with a dangling modifier occurs because the modifier has no subject of its own. The subject of the main clause is usually taken to be the subject of the modifier. This can create some ridiculous images:

> *On returning home*, the door slammed shut. (The door was not returning home.)
> *Falling from the tree*, the girl caught the apple. (The apple was falling from the tree, not the girl.)

Absolute constructions. Some modifiers, such as the adverb *thankfully* in "Thankfully, the rain stopped," modify an entire sentence. Certain phrases called *absolute constructions* work in a similar fashion:

> *The moment having arrived*, we went inside the courthouse.
> *The primary lost*, we abandoned our headquarters.

Such constructions are acceptable in English and should not be confused with dangling modifiers. Whereas absolute constructions modify an entire sentence, dangling modifiers modify the wrong elements in a sentence.

Parenthetical remarks. Occasionally you may want to insert a comment or explanation within a sentence. Such insertions are known as *parenthetical remarks*, and they may be punctuated with commas, parentheses, brackets, or dashes.

Commas are used only when the parenthetical remark is not a complete sentence, is very short, and flows well within the sentence:

My friend, *the one who moved to Chicago*, just got married.
John, *old and infirm though he is*, walked all the way home.

Commas are used in these sentences only for *nonrestrictive* phrases or clauses:

My daughter, *the doctor*, sent me a letter. (The writer has one daughter, who happens to be a doctor.)

When a sentence contains a *restrictive* clause or phrase, commas are not used:

My daughter *the doctor* sent me a letter. (The writer has more than one daughter. The one who is a doctor sent him the letter.)

Parentheses are used for longer material, full sentences, further explanation, and side comments:

The whole group (*except for those who had resigned*) agreed to settle the debt.
The article on cryogenics (*see page 38*) suggests that the future may hold great appeal for some sufferers.

Note that parentheses may be used for whole sentences as well as for words or phrases.

Brackets may be used in place of parentheses but are usually reserved for more formal situations:

. . . life, liberty, and the <u>pursuit</u> [*underline added*] of happiness.
The women live in purdah [*social seclusion as required by religion and custom*] and few men ever come in contact with them.

Dashes may be substituted for parentheses to set off a parenthetical remark:

The medium spoke of spirits—*poltergeists, ghosts, ghouls*—as if she thought we all believed in them.
A two-week camping trip—*whenever the weather allows us to leave*—will be the high point of our planned vacation.

The use of parentheses, brackets, or dashes is often a matter of personal choice. The important point is to be sure that the sentence written around the parenthetical remark makes sense in its own right. If you remove the parenthetical remark, the sentence should remain grammatically correct.

Sentence functions

Declarative sentences. A *declarative sentence* is a sentence that makes a statement. It ends with a period. In the following examples, the subject has been underlined and the verb has been italicized:

> The <u>horse</u> *was led* to the winner's circle.
> The <u>horse</u> *was led* to the winner's circle and a <u>blanket</u> of red roses *was draped* across its withers.
> The <u>horse</u>, which was named Stardust, *was led* to the winner's circle and a <u>blanket</u> of red roses *was draped* across its withers.

Interrogative sentences. An *interrogative sentence* is a sentence that asks a question. It ends with a question mark.

There are a limited number of words that can be used to begin an interrogative sentence. Some interrogative sentences begin with auxiliary verbs such as *is, do, are, can, may, have,* or *has.* The auxiliary verb comes before the subject. Often this means splitting the verb, with the auxiliary before the subject and the rest of the verb after the subject. The following examples show the auxiliary verb in italics and the main verb underlined:

> *Must* Ted and I <u>go</u> to the store right now?
> *Must* Ted and I <u>go</u> to the store right now or *may* we <u>go</u> in about an hour after we have finished roller-skating?

The main verbs *have* or *be* may be used without a second verb to begin an interrogative sentence. In such cases, the verb (italicized in the following sentences) comes before the subject:

> *Are* they at home?   *Have* you any wool?
> *Is* she a singer?   *Has* he a home?

Interrogative sentences may also begin with the words *who, what, where, when, how, why, which,* or *whose*:

> *Who* is coming to dinner?   *How* did they learn of it?
> *What* did he do?   *Why* hasn't Kerry written?
> *Where* are my socks?   *Which* house is yours?
> *When* will you leave?   *Whose* mess is that?

Indirect questions. An *indirect question* is not an interrogative sentence. Indirect questions are clauses that mention or suggest a question. Usually indirect questions are a part of declarative sentences and therefore end in periods. The examples below present three interrogative sentences followed by three declarative sentences containing indirect questions in italics:

> Where do they live?
> How much does it cost?
> Where did he find it?

> He asked me to find out *where they live*.
> Please find out *how much it costs*.
> She wondered *where he found it*.

The word order of an indirect question is not the normal word order used for an interrogative sentence. For example, "He asked me to find out where do they live" is not correct word order for an indirect question.

Exclamatory sentences. An *exclamatory sentence* is a sentence that expresses surprise, anger, or other strong emotion. It ends with an exclamation point:

> You did it!   Don't hit me!
> How good you are!   Stop!
> What a change!

Some words—*interjections*—are used chiefly in this type of sentence:

> Wow!   Phooey!

Note that exclamatory sentences do not need to have subjects and verbs. The word order may be the same as or different from that of a declarative sentence.

Imperative sentences. An *imperative sentence* is a sentence that makes a command or request. It ends in a period. The subject of an imperative sentence is always "you," which is usually understood without being expressed. Nevertheless, such a sentence is considered a complete sentence, as shown in the following examples:

> Bring me the book.
> Close your eyes and go to sleep.
> Please, tell me a story.

> Paul, take this money, go to the store, buy a loaf of bread, which we need for sandwiches, and give me the change.

Sentence fragments. A *sentence fragment* is a group of words that does not make a grammatical sentence. Often sentence fragments do not have a subject or a verb, or both; they are incomplete.

There are, however, many acceptable uses of sentence fragments:

Sentence fragments are acceptable as exclamations:

> What fun!   How lovely!

Sentence fragments are acceptable as questions, provided that a previous statement or question establishes the nature of the question:

> Mr. Smith is away on vacation.   *For how long?*
> He will be back soon.   *When?*

Sentence fragments are acceptable as answers to questions:

> Where did he go?   *Upstairs to his room.*
> Do you like him?   *No.*
> When will he return? *Next week.*

Sometimes writers use sentence fragments to accomplish a purpose—perhaps to establish a certain pace, or to suggest a disjointed quality. The chief danger of using sentence fragments lies in giving the impression that they are sentences. In business writing, therefore, it is best to avoid the use of sentence fragments. If you must use them, use them sparingly. The following example illustrates the errors that can occur when sentence fragments are incorrectly used:

> Strolling the ancient city's streets, I seem to hear the ghosts of history telling of its founding centuries ago. Of its trade with the Scythians and with tribes up and down the Danube. Telling of Alexander the Great.

Why is each of the last two word groupings a phrase rather than a sentence? Let us examine each of them:

> Of its trade with the Scythians and with tribes up and down the Danube.

This phrase has no verb and none of the nouns (*trade*, *Scythians*, *tribes*, *Danube*) is the subject. All the nouns are objects of prepositions.

> Telling of Alexander the Great.

The verb *telling* is the present participle of tell. But this verb is without a subject: the noun *Alexander the Great* is the object of a preposition.

There are several ways in which this paragraph can be changed to make all the fragments into sentences.

The entire paragraph can be rewritten as one sentence:

> Strolling the ancient city's streets, I seem to hear the ghosts of history telling of its founding centuries ago, of its trade with the Scythians and with tribes up and down the Danube, and also of Alexander the Great.

Or it can be rewritten by adding a subject to the two fragment sentences:

> Strolling the ancient city's streets, I seem to hear the ghosts of history telling of its founding centuries ago. The ghosts tell of trade with the Scythians and with tribes up and down the Danube. They also tell of Alexander the Great.

Sentence fragments may be long or short. If you recognize them for the incomplete sentences that they are, you will be able to use them or correct them as desired.

A paragraph consists of one or more sentences that introduce, develop, and conclude an idea about one subject. Each new paragraph explores a new idea, which is often stated in a paragraph's topic sentence. The remaining sentences in the paragraph expand on the topic sentence by giving specifics. The topic sentence is often, but not always, the first sentence of the paragraph.

Within a paragraph, the ideas contained in one sentence should logically develop from the ideas presented in the previous sentence. This progression should be clear and smooth and as apparent to the reader as it is to the writer.

What is true for each paragraph is also true for groups of paragraphs. There should be a clear, logical progression from paragraph to paragraph. Often the progression of ideas can be seen just by reading the topic sentences in each paragraph.

These are some general rules for developing paragraphs:

- Each paragraph should present a unit. It must be a grouping of sentences that are related to each other and to the main idea.
- Each paragraph should present a complete thought and expand on it fully before ending the paragraph and beginning the next.
- Within the paragraph, there should be a logical progression: from general to specific statements; from specific to general statements; from the beginning to the end of the action; from a statement to a refutation to a reexamination of the original statement. The possibilities are numerous.
- There should be a good balance of types of sentences. At times it works well to repeat the same structure in sentence after sentence within a paragraph. But this stylistic device can be overused. It is generally more effective to vary the rhythm, length, and construction of sentences.
- Maintain the same person throughout a paragraph. Switching from "you" to "one" to "they" can be disconcerting to your reader.
- Maintain the same tense for the same subject within a paragraph. Events in the past should not be described in the present and also in the past. At times, some of the events in a

paragraph may have taken place in the far past, others over a period of time. The sequence of tenses should make the time relationship clear.

Some paragraphs serve special functions within a written work and therefore require special attention.

The opening paragraph

The opening paragraph is the first paragraph of a written work. A major function of the opening paragraph is to engage the reader's attention. There are several customary ways of doing this:

- You can ask a question. The question should go to the heart of the material you deal with. The question may be asked as a direct question: "What weaving techniques were used by the indigenous peoples of the Yucatán?" or as an indirect question: "We wanted to know what weaving techniques were used by the indigenous peoples of the Yucatán."
- You can make a statement. The statement should be clearly worded. No qualifying phrases should offset the force of the statement. The statement may be the basic theme of the work or it may be the reason for writing the work: "There is no good published material on the weaving techniques used by the indigenous peoples of the Yucatán."
- You can begin with a quotation with which you agree or disagree. In either case, the quotation should be directly related to the theme of the work.
- You can present a short anecdote. The anecdote may be directly or obliquely related to the rest of the piece.
- You can cite an opinion by an authority or offer a common view with which you agree or disagree.

Transitional paragraphs

In a sense, every paragraph makes a transition from the paragraph that precedes it to the paragraph that follows. Some paragraphs, however, must make a major transition from one block of ideas to another block of ideas. You can use several devices to make transitions flow more smoothly:

- You can summarize what has gone before and lead in to the next theme by using a transitional word or phrase such as *moreover, on the other hand,* or *however.*
- You can use a short paragraph that picks up a word or phrase from the preceding paragraph, then introduce a main idea for what will follow.

The concluding paragraph

A concluding paragraph is the finishing touch to a piece of writing. It serves to tie together the sequence of ideas presented in the paragraphs and to give closure to the document by reemphasizing its main purpose. There are several ways this may be accomplished:

- You can summarize the ideas that have gone on before. This technique is effective only with long pieces of writing.
- You can draw conclusions about what has been said.
- You can state further questions to be explored at another time.
- You can end with a quotation from a respected authority on the subject.
- You can end with an anecdote that illustrates the main ideas of the document.

Correct word choice is essential to successful communication. Using the wrong word in conversation or written messages can lead to misunderstandings, and it can give the appearance of irresponsibility or ignorance. It makes sense therefore to be aware of the ways words are often misused. The usage notes that follow apply primarily to business, schools, government, and other institutions.

a, an *A* is used before a word beginning with a consonant (*a building*) or a consonant sound (*a university*); *an* is used before a word beginning with a vowel (*an employee*) or a vowel sound (*an hour*). Both *a* and *an* have been used before some words in which an initial *h* is pronounced in an unaccented syllable (*a historian*; *an historic occasion*). It is never wrong to use *a* in such situations, but *an* is often considered unacceptable. The best rule is to use *a* before all words beginning with *h* except those in which the *h* is not pronounced (*an honor*).

acquiesce When *acquiesce* takes a preposition, it is usually used with *in* (*acquiesced in the ruling*) but sometimes with *to* (*acquiesced to his mother's wishes*).

AD, BC, CE, BCE Traditionally in Western countries, events have been dated with reference to the birth of Jesus. In this system, the present epoch is designated by the letters AD, which stand for *anno Domini*, a Latin phrase meaning "in the year of the Lord." The epoch preceding the present epoch is designated in English with the letters BC, which stand for *before Christ*. The letters AD are usually put before the year number, but BC is put after, as in *The Roman Empire began in 31 BC after the battle of Actium and ended, in the West, in AD 476*. In light of a growing awareness of the beliefs of atheists and members of religious groups other than Christians, many writers now use another system of epoch names that contain no direct reference to Christianity. The current epoch is designated CE, standing for *common era*, while the epoch formerly designated BC is now designated BCE, standing for *before the common era*. Both CE and BCE follow the year. The abbreviations BC, AD, BCE, and CE have traditionally been written with periods as B.C., A.D., B.C.E., and C.E., but nowadays the periods are often omitted. Both styles are acceptable as long as consistency is maintained. The letters of all these abbreviations may be set in either small capitals or full capitals.

admission, admittance   *Admission* and *admittance* have traditionally been given different meanings. *Admission* means "achieving entry to a group or institution" (*her admission to the club*) whereas *admittance* means "obtaining physical access to a place" (*He was denied admittance to the courtroom*). Since *admission* also means "a fee paid for the right of entry," one pays *admission* to be allowed *admittance* to a theater.

adopted, adoptive   One refers to an *adopted* child but to *adoptive* parents, families, and homes.

advance, advancement   *Advance*, as a noun, is used for forward movement (*the advance of the army across the border*) or for progress or improvement in a figurative sense (*an advance in medicine*). *Advancement* is often used in the figurative sense to indicate promotion or movement beyond a norm: *There are a number of requirements for career advancement in my company.* In these uses *advancement* often implies the existence of an agent or outside force, but *advance* does not. Thus the *advance* of research means simply the progress of the company's efforts in research, whereas the *advancement* of research implies progress resulting from the action of an agent or force: *The addition of $1.5 million to the budget has resulted in the advancement of our research efforts.*

adverse   See **averse, adverse**.

advise   *Advise* in the sense "to give someone advice" is always acceptable: *The lawyer advised employees to observe the new regulations.* But the use of *advise* to mean "to inform, notify," as in *I would advise your friends that the date of the picnic has been changed*, often sounds pretentious and condescending.

affect, effect   *Affect* and *effect* have no sense in common. As a verb, *affect* is most commonly used in the sense "to influence": *How will bad weather affect deliveries? Effect* as a verb means "to bring about or execute": *The layoffs are designed to effect savings.* As a noun it means "a result": *The demonstration was one effect of* *the new policy.* Using *affect* in sentences like this will be viewed as a mistake.

affinity   *Affinity* may be followed by *of*, *between*, or *with*: *affinity of persons*, *affinity between two persons*, or *affinity with another person*. In technical writing *affinity*, meaning "a chemical or physical attraction," is followed by *for*: *This dye exhibits an affinity for synthetic fabrics.*

affirmative   The expressions *in the affirmative* and *in the negative* are generally regarded as pompous: *The professor answered in the affirmative.* A better expression would be a simpler one: *The professor answered yes.*

agenda   *Agenda,* meaning "a list or program," is well established as a singular noun. Its plural form is *agendas.*

ago   *Ago* may be followed by *that* or *when*: *It was a week ago that* (or *when*) *I saw Janine.* It should not be followed by *since*: *It was a week ago since my order arrived. Since* is properly used without *ago*: *It has been a week since my order arrived.*

alga, algae   *Alga* is a singular noun referring to a single organism or group of organisms. Its plural is *algae.* Sentences like *Toxic algae was growing in the water* are incorrect.

all   See **not.**

alleged   An *alleged* burglar is someone who is said to be a burglar but against whom no charges have yet been proved. An *alleged incident* is an event that is said to have taken place but which has not yet been verified. In their zeal to protect the rights of the accused, newspapers and law enforcement officials sometimes misuse *alleged.* A man arrested for murder may be only an *alleged murderer*, for example, but he is a real, not an *alleged*, *suspect* in that his status as a suspect is not in doubt.

all right, alright   The word *alright* is still considered an error in standard usage, despite the parallel to words like *already* and *altogether* and despite the fact that in casual speech the expression is often pronounced as if it were one word. Use *all right* instead in your formal written communications.

allude/allusion, refer/reference   *Allude* and *allusion* are often used where *refer* and *reference* would be more appropriate. *Allude* and *allusion* normally apply to an indirect reference: *He was alluding to her car accident when he asked if she had run into any old friends today*. *Refer* and *reference*, unless qualified, usually imply specific mention of something: *She made reference to the book in her speech*.

along with See **together with**.

alot Writing *a lot* as one word is a very common error in student writing and should be avoided in all standard contexts.

alternative *Alternative* is widely used to mean "one of a set of possible courses of action," but because the word comes from a Latin word meaning "the other of two," some people would restrict its use to situations in which only two possible choices present themselves: *The alternatives are to attend a traditional college or to enter a vocational school*. Under this stricter use, *alternative* is incompatible with all numerals (*There are three alternatives*), and even the use of *two* is unacceptable for being redundant (*The two alternatives are life and death*). For similar reasons, the familiar phrase *no other alternative* is often considered a redundancy.

altogether, all together *Altogether* should be distinguished from *all together*. *All together* is used with a group to indicate that its members performed or underwent an action collectively: *The new computers were stored all together in an empty office*. *All together* can be used only if it is possible to rephrase the sentence so that *all* and *together* may be separated by other words: *The new computers were all stored together*. *Altogether* is used to mean "entirely" or "completely": *It is altogether possible that we will lose the game*.

alumni *Alumni* is used to refer to male graduates of an institution. Female graduates are *alumnae*. When the graduates are of both sexes, traditional use allows the masculine form *alumni*, but some people require both terms in the interest of fairness, and others use the combined form *alumnae/i*. A good gender-neutral alternative is *graduates*.

AM/PM Strictly speaking, *12 AM* denotes midnight and *12 PM* denotes noon, but because there is so much confusion over these uses, it is better to use *12 midnight* and *12 noon*.

among   See **between, among**.

and   Although *and* has long been used to begin sentences, the practice tends to lend a conversational tone to what is written. It may be best to avoid this practice in business and legal writing, but it can have a dramatic effect, calling attention to the increased significance of the sentence that follows it. See also **but**.

and/or   Although *and/or* is widely used in business writing to mean "one or the other or both," this usage may be misunderstood, particularly in international correspondence, and can sound stilted.

anticipate, expect   Some traditionalists hold that *anticipate* should not be used simply as a synonym for *expect*. They restrict its use to senses in which it suggests some advance action, either to fulfill (*anticipate my desires*) or to forestall (*anticipate the competition's next move*). Others accept the word's use in the senses "to feel or realize beforehand" and "to look forward to" (often with the implication of foretasting pleasure): *They are anticipating* (or *expecting*) *a relaxing vacation.*

any   The pronoun *any* can take a singular or plural verb, depending on the meaning intended. It is acceptable to say *Any of these books is suitable*, where *any* means "any one of these books." It is also acceptable to say *Are any of these books available?* Here *any* means "one or more" or "some." The phrase *of any* is sometimes used in informal contexts to mean "of all": *That scientist is the best of any living authority on the subject.* However, many find this construction unacceptable. *Any* is also used to mean "at all" before a comparative adjective: *Are the field office reports any better this month?* The related use of *any* by itself to mean "at all" is informal and should be avoided in formal writing: *It didn't matter at all* (not *any*) *when they arrived.*

anyone, any one   The one-word form *anyone* (and the similar word *anybody*) is used to mean "whatsoever person or persons" and is always used with a singular verb: *Anyone who wants to can come along.* The two-word form *any one* is used to mean "whatever one (person or thing) of a group." *Anyone may join* means admission is open to everybody. *Any one may join* means admission is open to a single individual among the people who are applying for admission. When followed by *of,* only *any one* (two words) can be used: *Any one of them could do the job. Anyone* is often used in place of *everyone: Dale is the most thrifty person of anyone I know.* But the word *anyone* is unnecessary in this context: *Dale is the most thrifty person I know.*

apparent Used before a noun, *apparent* means "seeming": *Despite its apparent wealth, the college was deeply in debt.* Used after a form of the verb *to be,* however, *apparent* can mean either "seeming" (*The virtues of the writing program were only apparent*) or "obvious" (*The effects of the drought are apparent to anyone seeing the parched fields*). You should make sure that your intended meaning is clear from the context.

as . . . as, so . . . as Comparisons with *as . . . as* may be used in any context, positive or negative: *Their team is as good as ours.* The *so . . . as* construction is restricted to negative comparisons, especially when the word *not* is involved: *Their team is not so good as ours.*

as, since Both *as* and *since* can mean "because" or "inasmuch as." But *as* can also mean "at the same time that" and is sometimes misunderstood: *As they were leaving, she walked to the door.* The easiest way to avoid confusion is to use *since* when the meaning is "because": *Since they were leaving, she walked to the door.*

assure, ensure, insure *Assure, ensure,* and *insure* all mean "to make sure or certain." Only *assure* is used with reference to a person in the sense "to set the mind at rest": *They assured the president of their commitment.* Although *ensure* and *insure* have generally been used interchangeably, only *insure* is used in the commercial sense "to guarantee persons or property against risk." It is sensible therefore to use only *ensure* to mean "to make certain": *To ensure success, the company did a thorough market study.*

as well as *As well as* in the sense "in addition to" does not have the conjunctive force of *and.* Consequently, the singular subjects remain singular and govern singular verbs: *My niece, as well as most of her friends, attends the local college. As well as* is redundant in combination with both: *Both in theory as well as in practice, the idea is unsound.*

averse, adverse *Averse* and *adverse* are often confused. *Averse* indicates opposition or strong disinclination on the subject's part: *Andy was averse to joining the chess club.* *Adverse* refers to something that opposes or hinders progress: *Currently, banks must deal with an adverse economy. They proceeded, despite the adverse circumstances.*

aweigh See **way, under way, aweigh.**

awhile, a while *Awhile* is an adverb and is never preceded by a preposition such as *for*, but the two-word form *a while* may be preceded by a preposition. In writing, each of the following is acceptable: *stay awhile; stay for a while; stay a while* (but not *stay for awhile*).

back The expression *back of* is an informal variant of *in back of* and should be avoided in writing: *There was a small loading dock in back of* (not *back of*) *the factory.*

backward The adverb may be spelled *backward* or *backwards*, and the forms are interchangeable: *They each stepped backward in response to the noise; The mirror was facing backwards.* Only *backward* is an adjective: *The book presented a backward view of rural life.*

bacteria, bacterium The word *bacteria* is the plural of the noun *bacterium* and should always be used with a plural verb: *If the bacteria get into the bloodstream, they can cause severe illness.* Use of *bacteria* as a singular is a common mistake and should be avoided: *The bacteria produces deadly toxins.*

bad, badly Traditional usage requires the adjective *bad*, not *badly*, after linking verbs such as *feel* and *look*: *I felt bad* (not *badly*) *about missing the party.* Formal usage bans the use of *bad* and *good* as adverbs: *My tooth hurts badly* (not *bad*). *He drives well* (not *good*).

baleful, baneful *Baleful* and *baneful* overlap in meaning, but *baleful* usually applies to that which menaces or foreshadows evil. *Baneful* is used most often for that which is actually harmful or destructive: *Although the baneful effects of littering in public parks are well-known, many people still fail to deposit trash in waste containers.*

BC, BCE See **AD, BC, CE, BCE**.

beside, besides The senses "in addition to" and "except for" are conveyed more often by *besides* than *beside*: *We had few options besides the course we ultimately took. Beside*, as a preposition, usually means "next to": *His computer is positioned beside the printer.* Watch out for ambiguity with *beside*: *There was no one beside me at the table.* This sentence means that the seats next to you were not occupied but could be misinterpreted to mean that you were alone. See also **together with**.

better, best In standard usage *better* is used in a comparison of two: *Which of the two accounting firms does the better job? Best* is used to compare three or more: *Which of these four methods works best? Best* is also used idiomatically with reference to two in certain expressions: *May the best team win!*

between, among *Between* is used when two entities are involved: *the rivalry between the Yankees and the Red Sox.* When more than two entities are involved, the choice of *between* or *among* depends on the intended meaning. *Among* is used to indicate that an entity has been chosen from the members of a group: *Among the three candidates, Sarah seems most likely to become the next president. Among* is also used to indicate a relation of inclusion in a group: *He is among the best songwriters of our time. Between* is used to indicate the area bounded by several points: *We have narrowed the search to the area between Philadelphia, New York, and Scranton.* In other cases either *between* or *among* may be used, but with a subtle difference in meaning. Thus if a hot-air balloon comes down *among* the houses, it lands in the area of the houses, and possibly on top of one. If it comes down *between* the houses, it lands in the space between the houses, hitting none.

bimonthly, semimonthly *Bimonthly* and *biweekly* mean "once every two months" and "once every two weeks." For "twice a month" and "twice a week," the words *semimonthly* and *semiweekly* should be used. But there is a great deal of confusion over the distinction, and a writer is well advised to substitute expressions like "every two months" or "twice a month" whenever possible. However, the word *bimonthly* is unavoidable when used as a noun to mean "a publication that appears every two months."

blatant, flagrant   *Blatant* and *flagrant* are similar in meaning but often confused. *Blatant* means "totally or offensively conspicuous" and emphasizes the actor's failure to conceal the act. *Flagrant* means "conspicuously offensive" and emphasizes the serious wrongdoing inherent in the offense. Therefore, one who blunders may be guilty of a *blatant* (but not a *flagrant*) error; one who intentionally and ostentatiously violates a pledge commits a *flagrant* act.

born, borne   In its literal sense the past participle *born* is used only in passive constructions (using a form of *be*) relating to birth: *The baby was born today. Born* may also be used figuratively: *Out of that meeting a great project was born. Borne* is used for all other senses of *bear,* including the act of giving birth: *She has borne three children. The soil has borne abundant crops. Such a burden cannot be borne by anyone.*

borrow   In spoken English, people sometimes use the expression *borrow off* in place of *borrow from.* In written contexts use only *borrow from: Gale borrowed $500 from* (not *off*) *the bank.*

both   *Both* indicates that the action or state denoted by a verb applies equally to two entities. Saying that *both* packages weigh more than five pounds means that each package weighs more than five pounds by itself. When used in conjunction with certain words, *both* is redundant. It is unnecessary to say they are *both alike,* since neither could be "alike" if the other were not. Similarly, *both* is unnecessary in a sentence saying that they *both* appeared together, since neither one can "appear together" individually. In possessive constructions, *of both* is usually preferred in standard contexts: *the works of both authors* (rather than *both their works*).

bring, take   *Bring* usually denotes movement toward the place of speaking or the point from which the action is regarded: *Bring the letter to me now. Take* denotes movement away from such a place. Thus you normally *take* checks to the bank and *bring* home cash, though from the banker's point of view, you have *brought* checks to the bank in order to *take* away cash.

burgeon The verb *burgeon* and its participle *burgeoning*, used as an adjective, are traditionally restricted to the actual or the figurative sense "to bud or sprout" or "to emerge": *The burgeoning talent of the young cellist was apparent to all.* *Burgeon* is not normally considered a synonym for the more general *expand, grow,* or *thrive*: *The burgeoning population of Seattle presents some problems for city planners.* This use of the present participle has become more acceptable in recent years, however.

but *But* is sometimes used as a preposition to mean "except" and so pronouns that follow it should be in the objective case: *No one but me can read it.* *But* is redundant when combined with *however*: *But the division, however, went on with its own plans.* Using *but* when it means "no more than" or "only" is unnecessary in negative sentences: *It won't take but an hour.* The expression *but what* is not normally used in standard writing: *I don't know but what (whether) we'll arrive first.* Similarly, standard practice bans the use of *but* instead of *than* in this type of sentence: *It no sooner started but (than) it stopped.* Beginning a sentence with *but* is now widely accepted, even in business English. See also **and**.

cache, cachet These words are sometimes confused. The word *cache* rhymes with *cash* and refers to a store of goods kept in a hiding place: *The police found a cache of drugs in the apartment.* The word *cachet* is pronounced with two syllables to rhyme with *sashay* and means "distinction or prestige associated with something": *He drove the sports car because of its cachet.*

callous, callus The noun is spelled *callus* (a *callus* on my foot), but the adjective is spelled *callous*: *The pickpocket showed a callous disregard for the feelings of his victims.*

can, may By tradition, *can* should be used only to express the capacity to do something and *may* to indicate permission: *The supervisor said that anyone who wants an extra day off may have one. May I have that pencil?* In informal speech, however, *can* is often used to express permission. The negative contraction *can't* is frequently used in questions, probably because *mayn't* sounds unnatural: *Can't I have the car tonight?* The increased formality of *may* sometimes highlights the role of the speaker in giving permission: *You may leave the room when you are finished.* Using *can* in a sentence like this implies that permission is part of a rule or policy rather than a decision on the part of the speaker.

cannot   In the phrase *cannot but*, which is criticized as a double negative, *but* is used in the sense of "except": *You cannot but admire the view* (you cannot do otherwise than admire the view). Alternative phrasings are *can but admire, can only admire, cannot help admiring.*

capital, capitol   The term for a town or city that serves as a seat of government is spelled *capital*. The term for the building in which a legislative assembly meets is spelled *capitol*. It is capitalized (*Capitol*) in references to the seat of the US Congress.

center   As a verb *center* is used with *on, upon, in,* or *at: Our thoughts centered on the flood victims. The business is centered in New York.* Traditionalists maintain that *center* should not be used with *around*, since the word *center* refers to a point of focus: *The discussion centered on* (not *around*) *the meaning of the law.* Alternatives to *center around* include *revolve around, focus on, concern,* or *involve: The discussion focused on the meaning of the law.*

ceremonial, ceremonious   *Ceremonial* (adjective) is applicable chiefly to things; *ceremonious* (also an adjective), to persons and things. *Ceremonial* means simply "having to do with ceremony": *There were many ceremonial occasions for the family this year. Ceremonial garb was required at the ritual. Ceremonious*, when applied to a person, means "devoted to forms and ritual" or "standing on ceremony": *She was regarded as a ceremonious chief of protocol.*

certain   *Certain* is sometimes claimed to be an absolute term like *unique.* Under this thinking something is either certain, or it is not, and expressions like *more certain* and *fairly certain* are unacceptable. Nonetheless, modification of *certain* in this way is widespread in the writing of the most respected writers and cannot be considered incorrect. Note, however, that because *certain* suggests confidence, its modification by undercutting words like *slightly, somewhat,* and *a little bit* is uncommon and sounds unnatural.

cite   See **quote, cite.**

commentate The verb *commentate* has long been in use in the sense "to give a commentary" and more recently in the sense "to provide a running commentary on": *The announcer commentated (or commentated on) the tennis tournament.* Many people find *commentate* awkward or pretentious, however, and prefer the simpler *comment on* or *give a commentary on*.

common See **mutual, common**.

compare, contrast *Compare* means "to examine something for similarity or difference" and is followed by *to* or *with*. Use *to* when you want to highlight the similarity between things: *People often compare the human brain to a computer.* Use *with* when you examine two things for similarities or differences: *We compared the original with the copy to see if there were any discrepancies.* The verb *contrast* means "to be different" or "to show differences in." It is often followed by *with*: *The senator's views contrast sharply with his predecessor's. We contrasted the new plan with the old one.* As a noun *contrast* is often followed by *to*, though *between* and *with* are also acceptable: *My cousins, in contrast to me and my brothers, are fluent in both English and Spanish. We all agreed that there was a strong contrast between the two offers. By contrast with the fancy new kitchen, the rest of the house seemed drab.*

complement, compliment *Complement* and *compliment*, though distinct in meaning, are sometimes confused because they are pronounced the same. *Complement* means "something that completes or brings to perfection": *The ornate carpet was a perfect complement to the expensive furniture. Compliment* means "an expression of courtesy or praise": *She received many compliments on her winning essay.*

complete *Complete* is generally held to be an absolute term like *perfect* or *chief*, words that are not supposed to be subject to comparison. Nevertheless, *complete* is commonly qualified by *more* or *less*: *I could not imagine a more complete failure. That book is the most complete treatment of the subject available today.* Sentences like these are acceptable in all contexts.

comprise, compose The traditional rule states that the whole *comprises* the parts; the parts *compose* the whole: *The Union comprises 50 states. Fifty states compose* (or *constitute* or *make up*) the

Union. However, *comprise* is often used, especially in the passive, in place of *compose: The Union is comprised of 50 states*. This construction lends a more formal tone to a piece of writing in spite of the fact that it violates the traditional rule.

continuance, continuation, continuity *Continuance* is sometimes interchangeable with *continuation*. *Continuance*, however, is used to refer to the duration of a state or condition: *The president's continuance in office was troubling to some people*. *Continuation* applies especially to prolongation or resumption of action (*This meeting is a continuation of the council meeting*) or to physical extension (*The continuation of the railroad spur beyond our town means more rail traffic throughout the day*). *Continuity* is used to refer to consistency over time: *The continuity of foreign policy was secured by her appointment*. The *continuity* of a story is its internal coherence from one episode to the next; the *continuation* of a story is that part of the story that takes up after a break in its recitation.

contrast See **compare, contrast**.

convince, persuade Traditionally, one *persuades* someone to act but *convinces* someone of the truth of a statement or proposition: *By convincing me that I was as qualified as the other applicants, the guidance counselor persuaded me to try for the scholarship*. If the distinction is accepted, then *convince* should not be used with an infinitive: *They persuaded* (not *convinced*) *me to go*. Nevertheless, *convince* is used with an infinitive in the most prestigious publications and must be considered standard.

council, counsel, consul *Council*, *counsel*, and *consul* are never interchangeable, although their meanings are related. *Council* and *councilor* refer principally to a deliberative assembly (a *city council* or *student council*) and one of its members. *Counsel* and *counselor* pertain chiefly to advice and guidance and to a person who provides it: *We're proceeding according to the counsel of our attorney*. *Consul* denotes an officer in the foreign service of a country: *The consul in Bogotá was welcomed by the country's new leaders*.

criteria, criterion *Criteria* is a plural form only (*The criteria for making a decision are clear*) and should not be substituted for the singular *criterion: His sole criterion for opposing the project is its cost*.

critique   *Critique* is widely used as a verb (*critiqued the survey*) but is regarded by many as pretentious jargon. The use of it as a noun in phrases like *give a critique* or *offer a critique* is acceptable. Better still might be to use another verb, such as *analyze, go over,* or *review.*

data   Although *data* is the plural of the Latin word *datum,* it is usually treated as a singular noun: *The data is inconclusive.* Using a plural verb with *data* is also acceptable, though it tends to impart a more formal or scientific tone.

depend   *Depend,* indicating condition or contingency, is always followed by *on* or *upon: It depends on who is in charge.* In casual speech the preposition is sometimes omitted: *It depends (on) who is in charge.*

deprecate, depreciate   The traditional meaning of *deprecate* is "to express disapproval of," but over the years the word has taken on the traditional meaning of *depreciate,* probably by influence of the adjective *self-deprecating,* and is now used to mean "to belittle or mildly disparage": *The winner of the award deprecated his own contributions as no better than anyone else's. Depreciate* has also seen its traditional sense become less common, and today it is used primarily in financial contexts to mean "to fall in price or value": *The value of a car depreciates immediately after you purchase it.*

different from, different than   A traditional rule states that *different than* should never be followed by a noun or noun phrase, only by a clause: *The campus is different than it was the last time you were here. Different from* is required for nouns and noun phrases: *My book is different from yours. Living in an apartment is quite different from living in a dormitory.* While this distinction is often ignored in informal settings, it remains a mainstay of copyediting lore, and so should be observed in more formal situations.

dilemma   *Dilemma* applies to a choice between evenly balanced alternatives, often unattractive ones: *He faced the dilemma of choosing between a higher salary in another state or a lower salary close to home.* It is not properly used as a synonym for *problem* or *predicament: Shoplifting has become a big problem* (not *dilemma*) *for this supermarket.*

discreet, discrete   These words sound alike and are related to each other etymologically, but they have different meanings. *Discreet* means "prudent in speech and behavior": *He told me the news but asked me to be discreet about it.* *Discrete* means "separate, distinct": *The summer science program consists of four discrete units.*

disinterested, uninterested   Traditionally, a *disinterested* party is one who has no stake in a dispute and is therefore presumed to be impartial. One is *uninterested* in something when one is indifferent to it. Although *disinterested* is sometimes used in popular writing where *uninterested* is meant, the distinction between these terms is a useful one and should be maintained: *I volunteered to find a disinterested person to settle the argument, but everyone I asked was uninterested.*

distinct, distinctive   A thing is *distinct* if it is sharply distinguished from other things: *a distinct honor.* A property or attribute is *distinctive* if it enables us to distinguish one thing from another. If a bird has two *distinct* colors on its wings, it has two colors that are sharply different from each other. If it has two *distinctive* colors, it has colors that are different from the colors on the wings of birds of other species, and the bird may be identified by these colors.

done   *Done* means "completely accomplished" or "finished": *The entire project will not be done until next year.* In some contexts, however, this use of *done* can be unclear: *The work will be done next week.* Does that mean that it will be finished next week or that someone will do the work next week? Alternatives, dependent on the meaning, would be *The work will get done next week* or *The work will be done by next week.*

doubt, doubtful   *Doubt* and *doubtful* are often followed by clauses introduced by *that, whether,* or *if.* Often *that* is used when the intention is to show a negative expectation or to reject what has been suggested: *I doubt that he will even try to clean up his room.* In the negative *doubt* is often used to express more or less complete acceptance: *I don't doubt that you are right.* When the intention is to express real uncertainty, *whether* is the best choice for formal contexts: *We doubt whether they can succeed.* If and *that* are also acceptable, though they are more informal in tone. Most informal is to omit *that: I doubt they will succeed. Doubt* is frequently used in informal speech, both as a verb and as a noun, together with *but: I don't doubt but* (or *but that*) *they will come.* However, many people find the use of *but* here awkward, and it can be omitted with no loss in meaning.

drunk, drunken   As an adjective *drunk* is generally used after the verb *be* or *seem: The waiter seemed drunk.* Before a noun, the choice is usually *drunken: A drunken guest started an argument.* The use of *drunk* before a noun is informal and generally unacceptable in standard usage except in the phrases *drunk driver* and *drunk driving.*

due, due to   The phrase *due to* is always acceptable when *due* functions as a predicate adjective following a linking verb: *Our hesitancy was due to fear.* Some language critics have insisted that *due* is used improperly as an adverb when *due to* follows a non-linking verb, even though this usage is widespread in standard contexts: *The game was canceled due to the rain. We hesitated due to fear.* Generally accepted substitutes for this construction include *because of* or *on account of.*

each   When the subject of a sentence begins with *each*, it is grammatically singular, and the verb and following pronouns must be singular as well: *Each of the apartments has its own private entrance.* When *each* follows a plural subject, however, the verb and following pronouns generally remain plural: *The editors each have their jobs to do.*

each other, one another   Traditionally, *each other* refers to two, and *one another* refers to more than two: *Bob and Jane wrote to each other. The nurses help one another.* When speaking of an ordered series of events or stages, only *one another* can be used: *The Caesars exceeded one another in cruelty* means that each Caesar was crueler than the previous one. *Each other* should not be used as the subject of a clause: *We know what each other are thinking.* A better construction would be *Each of us knows what the other is thinking.* The possessive forms of *each other* and *one another* are written *each other's* and *one another's: The miners inspected one another's gear.*

effect See **affect, effect.**

either Traditionally, *either* is used only to refer to one of two items, and *any* or *any one* is used to refer to more than two: *Either of the teams could score in the next period. Any of the three candidates has a chance at winning.* Whether used as a pronoun or an adjective, *either* normally takes a singular verb: *I doubt whether either of the books is available. Either plant grows well in the shade.* An exception is when *either* is part of an *either/or* construction that consists of plural subjects: *Either the children or the dogs are making that thumping noise.*

elder When used as an adjective in comparisons between two persons, *elder* is simply a more formal term for "older" and has no implication of advanced age: *My elder sibling is fourteen; my younger is nine.* In other contexts it does denote relatively old age, but with the added component of respect for a person's position or achievement: *an elder statesman, an elder member of the court.* If the simple fact of advanced or relatively advanced age is the point, *older* or *elderly* are usually more appropriate than *elder: a survey of older Americans, an elderly waiter.*

As with the adjective, the noun *elder* can be used comparatively without implying old age: *He is my elder by three years.* It can also refer to an office in certain churches or, more broadly, to a position of authority or respect conferred by age and experience: *an elder in the Presbyterian Church, a tribal elder.* The use of *elder* in the sense of "an elderly person" is uncommon in contemporary English, though it is widely used as an attributive in such phrases as *elder care* (or *eldercare*) and *elder services.*

elderly *Elderly* applies to the stage of life well past middle age and suggests greater age than the similar term *older: An elderly couple lives around the corner. The older people in the neighborhood are generally in favor of the proposal.* When used as a noun in referring to older persons in general, *elderly* is relatively neutral, denoting a group of people whose common characteristic is advanced age: *policy issues of special interest to the elderly.*

else *Else* is often used redundantly in combination with prepositions such as *but, except,* and *besides: No one* (not *no one else*) *but that witness saw the accident.* When a pronoun is followed by *else,* the possessive form is generally written as *someone else's* (not *someone's else*). Both *who else's* and *whose else* are in use, but not *whose else's*: *Who else's notebook could it have been? Whose else could it have been?*

emigrate See **migrate, emigrate, immigrate**.

enormity, enormousness *Enormity* has traditionally been used to refer to the events or actions worthy of a strong negative moral judgment: *The citizens were appalled at the enormity of the government's brutal response.* As such, *enormity* should not be used to mean "largeness, immensity." In these cases *enormousness* works well: *The engineers were not daunted by the enormousness of the task before them.* In fact, in some contexts, using *enormity* to mean "immensity" can lead to unintentionally comic ambiguities: *the enormity of the governor's campaign funding.*

ensure See **assure, ensure, insure**.

errata The plural *errata* is sometimes employed in the collective sense of a list of errors. Nevertheless, *errata* always takes a plural verb: *The errata are noted in an attached memo.*

every *Every* takes a singular verb: *Every student in the school is expected to be on time.* Because it is singular, *every* can make trouble for writers who want to avoid pronouns that could imply sexism: *Every student must empty his locker by Thursday.* An alternative is to use *their* instead of *his* and break the traditional rule about pronoun agreement. An easier solution is to avoid *every* in such sentences by writing in the plural: *All students must empty their lockers by Thursday.*

everyplace, every place *Everyplace* and *every place* used adverbially for *everywhere* are found principally in informal writing or speech: *Everyplace* (or *every place*) *I go, I hear raves about that movie.* A better construction would be *Everywhere I go, I hear raves about that movie. Every place* as a combination of adjective and noun is standard English: *I searched in every place possible.*

except *Except* in the sense "with the exclusion of" or "other than" is generally construed as a preposition, not a conjunction. A personal pronoun that follows *except* is therefore in the objective case: *No one except them knew it. Every guest arrived late except me.*

expect   See **anticipate, expect.**

explicit, express   *Explicit* and *express* both apply to something that is clearly stated rather than implied. *Explicit* applies more particularly to that which is carefully spelled out: *The explicit requirements for graduating early are contained in the school handbook. Express* applies particularly to a clear expression of intention or will: *The corporation made an express prohibition against dealers selling cars below list prices.*

farther, further   Traditionally, *farther* is used for physical distance: *The freight train went farther down the line. Further* is used for metaphorical advancement, as when referring to degree or time: *The accident pushed us further into debt. The company took further steps to advertise its product.* In some cases, however, especially in contemporary writing, either word is acceptable. You may say *further from the truth* or *farther from the truth.*

faze, phase   The verb *faze* comes from Old English and means "to disrupt the composure of, disconcert." It is usually used in negative contexts, as in *She was not fazed by the setback but carried on as determined as ever. Faze* is sometimes mistakenly spelled *phase,* which is both a noun and a verb that is derived from Greek. The noun means "a stage of development." The verb usually occurs in the phrases *phase in* and *phase out,* which mean introducing or ending something one stage at a time.

fewer, less   *Fewer* refers to a number that is smaller when compared to another number. As such, it is correctly used in writing only before a plural noun: *There were fewer gains on the stock market today than yesterday. Fewer houses sold this month. Less* refers to a mass or collection and is used before singular nouns that can't be used in the plural: *There was less music in the second program. We had less trouble with the new puppy.* But sometimes plural amounts are considered to be singular masses (*$500 is a lot of money*), and *less* is therefore acceptable when used before a plural noun that denotes a measure of time, amount, or distance: *It has been less than three weeks since the announcement. The ski equipment cost less than $400. It is less than 50 miles to Biloxi.*

finalize   *Finalize* has long been associated with business jargon: *We will finalize plans to remodel 12 stores this year.* The word is often avoided by many writers in non-business contexts. The word has no exact synonym, though approximate substitutes include *complete, finish, make final,* and *put into final form.*

flagrant See **blatant, flagrant.**

flammable, inflammable *Flammable* and *inflammable* are identical in meaning. *Flammable* has been adopted by safety authorities for the labeling of combustible materials because the *in–* of *inflammable* was incorrectly believed by some people to mean "not": *The liquid is flammable.*

flaunt, flout *Flaunt* and *flout* are often confused. *Flaunt* as a transitive verb means "to exhibit ostentatiously": *The champion flaunted a gold-plated trophy.* To *flout* means "to show contempt for" or "to defy openly." It usually has a word like *rules, tradition,* or *convention* for its object: *They flouted all social proprieties.*

flounder See **founder, flounder.**

forceful, forcible, forced *Forceful, forcible,* and *forced* have distinct, if related, meanings. *Forceful* is used to describe something that suggests strength or force: *a forceful argument. Forceful* measures may or may not involve the use of actual physical force. *Forcible* is most often used concerning actions accomplished by the application of physical force: *There had clearly been a forcible entry into the storeroom. The suspect had to be forcibly restrained. Forced* is used to describe a condition brought about by control or by an outside influence: *Products made by forced labor are generally shunned in the international marketplace. It became necessary for the pilot to make a forced landing. Her displeasure was evident in her forced smile.*

forgo, forego The verb *forgo,* meaning "to abstain from, do without," has as an acceptable variant the spelling *forego.* Thus, one can *forgo* or *forego* dessert, though the spelling without the *e* is far more common and is preferred in most dictionaries. *Forego* also exists as a separate word meaning "to go before, either in place or time," as in *A bad reputation often foregoes you.*

former The word *former* is used when referring to the first of two persons or things mentioned: *If I had to choose between an analog and a digital watch, I would choose the former.* The second person or thing is referred to as *the latter*. It is best not to use *former* when referring to the first of three or more. For that purpose one may use *the first* or *the first-named* or, preferably, repeat the name itself: *Computers, scanners, and copiers are integrated in many offices, with computers representing the dominant technology.*

fortuitous, fortunate *Fortuitous* is often confused with *fortunate*. Traditionally, *fortuitous* means "happening by chance." *Fortunate* means "having unexpected good fortune." Thus, a *fortuitous* meeting may have either fortunate or unfortunate consequences. But because of similarity in sound *fortuitous* often carries an implication of lucky chance rather than unlucky chance. To avoid being misunderstood, careful writers should make clear in the context which meaning of *fortuitous* is intended. Note that *fortuitous* always means "lucky" when it is modified by an adverb like *very* or *somewhat*.

forward, forwards *Forwards* should not be used in place of *forward* except in the adverbial sense of "toward the front": *The bus driver asked the passenger to move forward* (or *forwards*). In specific phrases the choice of one or the other is often idiomatic: *Look forward. Her life changed from that day forward. The seaweed moved backward and forward as dictated by the movement of the water.*

founder, flounder The verbs *founder* and *flounder* are often confused. *Founder* comes from a Latin word meaning "bottom" (*foundation*) and originally referred to knocking enemies down; it is now used to mean "to sink below the water" and "to fail utterly, collapse." *Flounder* means "to move clumsily; thrash about," and hence "to proceed in confusion." *If the railroad's business between Chicago and Peoria founders, expect the line to be shut down; if the restaurant is floundering, longer hours and lower prices may still save it.*

fulsome *Fulsome* is often used, especially in the phrase *fulsome praise*, as the equivalent of *full and abundant*. This could lead to possible confusion because of the sense "offensively flattering or insincere"; hence *fulsome praise* could be taken to mean insincere, unctuous compliments.

further See **farther, further**.

good, well   *Good* is used as an adjective with linking verbs such as *be, seem,* or *appear: The future looks good. Well* should be used as an adverb: *The motor runs well.*

got, gotten   *Gotten* is considered by many to be an illegitimate "nonword," but it is actually very useful because of its subtleties in meaning. *Got* often implies current possession, where *gotten* usually suggests the process of obtaining. Accordingly, *I haven't got any money* suggests that one is broke, while *I haven't gotten any money* suggests that one hasn't been paid. This sense of process or progression applies to many other uses of *gotten,* and in some of these cases *got* just doesn't sound as natural to the American ear: *The bridge has gotten weaker since the storm. We have finally gotten used to the new software. Mice have gotten into the basement.* Remember that only *got* can be used to express obligation, as in *I've got to go to Chicago.* The sentence *I have gotten to go to Chicago* implies that the person has had the opportunity or been given permission to go.

government   In American usage *government* always takes a singular verb: *The government is too bureaucratic.* In British usage *government,* in the sense of a governing group of officials, is usually construed as a plural collective and therefore takes a plural verb: *The government are determined to maintain strict reins on industry.*

group   *Group* as a collective noun can be followed by a singular or plural verb. It takes a singular verb when the persons or things that make up the group are considered collectively: *The group is ready to present its report. Group* takes a plural verb when the persons or things that make it up are considered individually: *The group were divided in their loyalties.*

half   The phrases *a half, half of,* and *half a* are all correct, though they may differ slightly in meaning. For example, *a half day* is used when *day* has the special sense "a working day," and the phrase then means "4 hours." *Half of a day* and *half a day* are not restricted in this way and can mean either 4 or 12 hours. When the accompanying word is a pronoun, however, the phrase with *of* must be used: *half of them.* The phrase *a half a* is unacceptable in standard usage.

hanged   *Hanged*, as the past tense and past participle of *hang*, is properly used in the sense "put to death by hanging": *Frontier courts hanged* (not *hung*) *many a prisoner after a summary trial*. In all other senses of the word, *hung* is the preferred form as past tense and past participle: *He hung the calendar by his desk*.

hardly   *Hardly* has the force of a negative; therefore, it is not used with another negative: *I could hardly see* (not *couldn't hardly see*). A clause following *hardly* is introduced by *when* or, less often, by *before*: *We had hardly finished one report when* (or *before*) *another was assigned*. Such a clause is not introduced by *than* in formal style: *Hardly had I walked inside when* (not *than*) *the downpour started*.

he   Traditionally, the pronouns *he, him,* and *his* are used as generic singular pronouns in formal writing: *No one seems to take pride in his work anymore*. This usage has been criticized as sexist, however, and writers have developed numerous strategies to avoid it. One is to use compound pronouns such as *he or she* and *she/he*. These are acceptable but often cumbersome. Another strategy is to alternate generic *he* with generic *she*, in chapters, paragraphs, or even sentences if the subject matter will allow it. A solution that is very common in speech is to use *they, their,* and *them* to refer to singular nouns and pronouns: *Everyone must finish their work on time*. This practice violates the grammatical rule of number agreement for pronouns, but many choose to employ it anyway. Perhaps the best solution is to write consistently in the plural: *All employees must finish their work on time*.

headquarters   As a noun *headquarters* is properly used with either a singular or a plural verb. A plural verb is more common: *The committee's headquarters are upstairs*. But a singular verb is sometimes preferred when reference is to authority rather than to physical location: *Headquarters has approved the purchase of desktop computers for our engineers*.

help   *Help* in the sense "avoid" or "refrain from" is frequently used in an expression such as *I cannot help but think*. Other ways of saying the same thing include *I cannot help thinking* and *I cannot but think*. Another idiomatic use of *help* is exemplified by this sentence: *Don't change it any more than you can help* (any more than you have to). Some grammarians condemn this usage on the ground that *help* in this sense means "avoid" and logically requires a negative, but the expression is well established.

here In constructions introduced by *here is* and *here are*, the number of the verb is governed by the subject, which appears after the verb: *Here is the cake I promised to bring. Here are the cupcakes I promised to bring.*

historic, historical *Historic* and *historical* are differentiated in usage, although their senses overlap. *Historic* refers to what is important in history: *the historic first voyage to outer space.* It is also used in regard to what is famous or interesting because of its association with persons or events in history: *Frederick Douglass's home is considered to be a historic site.* *Historical* refers to whatever existed in the past, whether regarded as important or not: *The novel contained several historical characters.* Events are *historical* if they happened, *historic* only if they are regarded as important. *Historical* refers also to anything concerned with history or the study of the past: *The city supports its historical society well. He was well known for his historical novels.*

hoard, horde These two words sound alike and can be confused. A *hoard* is a hidden fund or supply stored for future use; to *hoard* something is to gather or accumulate a *hoard* of it. The noun *horde* is used to refer to any large group, especially a crowd or swarm. There is no verb *horde*. Thus *hoard* is used primarily of things, while *horde* applies to people and other living things (such as insects). Only a *horde* of reporters should follow a movie star around, never a *hoard*. When large numbers of people are turning up in different places, the plural *hordes* is common: *hordes of students returning to campus, hordes of volunteers helping to get out the vote.*

hopefully The use of *hopefully* to mean "it is to be hoped" (*Hopefully, we'll exceed last year's sales volume*) can be justified by analogy to the similar uses of *happily* and *mercifully*. However, it may be best to avoid using *hopefully* this way because many people consider it an error.

horde See **hoard, horde**.

how   The use of *as how* for *that* (*They said as how they would go*) is not considered standard and should be avoided. For similar reasons, the expressions *seeing as how* and *being as how* should also be avoided in formal writing.

however   *However* is redundant in combination with *but*. One or the other should be used: *We had an invitation but didn't go. We had an invitation; however, we didn't go.* The use of *however* as the first word of a sentence is generally acceptable.

identical   Some language critics insist that *with* is the preferred preposition after *identical*. But both *with* and *to* are acceptable: *This year's model is identical with* (or *to*) *last year's.*

if   *If* may be substituted for *whether* to introduce a clause indicating uncertainty after a verb such as *ask, doubt, know, learn,* or *see: We shall soon learn if* (or *whether*) *it is true. If* should be avoided when it may be ambiguous: *Please inform the registrar if you intend to be present.* (Does it mean *whether or not* you intend to be present or *only if* you intend to be present?) Often *if not* is also ambiguous: *The discovery offered persuasive, if not conclusive, evidence.* This could mean "persuasive and perhaps conclusive" or "persuasive but not conclusive." Traditionally, the subjunctive (*if I were*) is used for a situation contrary to fact: *If I were the president, I would* (or *should*) *make June 1 a national holiday.* The indicative is required when the situation described by the *if* clause is assumed to be true: *If I was short with you a moment ago, it is only because I wasn't paying attention.* When an *if* clause is preceded by *ask* or *wonder*, use the indicative: *He asked if Napoleon was a great general.* Using *would have* in place of the subjunctive in contrary-to-fact *if* clauses is incorrect: *If I had been* (not *If I would have been*) *promoted.*

immigrate   See **migrate, emigrate, immigrate**.

impact   As a verb *impact* is sometimes used transitively: *These taxes impact small businesses.* It is also used intransitively with *on: These policies have impacted on our ability to achieve success.* Many language critics object to these usages as typical of bureaucratic jargon.

imply   See **infer, imply**.

impracticable, impractical The adjective *impracticable* applies to a course of action that is impossible to carry out or put into practice: *Refloating the sunken ship proved to be impracticable because of its fragility. Impractical* can also be used in this way, but it also has a weaker sense, suggesting that the course of action would yield an insufficient return, have little practical value, or be difficult to carry out. A plan for a new baseball stadium might be rejected as *impracticable* if the site was too marshy to permit safe construction, but if the objection were merely that the site was too remote for patrons to attend games easily, the plan would better be described as *impractical.*

in addition to See **together with**.

infer, imply The words *infer* and *imply* should not be confused. When a speaker or sentence *implies* something, information is conveyed or suggested without being stated outright: *When the mayor said that she would not rule out a tax increase, she implied* (not *inferred*) *that some taxes might be raised.* To *infer* something, on the other hand, is to draw conclusions that are not explicit in what is said. It is the activity of a reader or listener: *When the mayor said that she would not rule out a tax increase, we inferred that she had been consulting new financial advisers, since her old advisers were in favor of tax reductions.*

inflammable See **flammable, inflammable**.

injustice, unjust Usually the prefixes in the negatives of adjectives correspond to those in their noun forms, as in *indiscreet* and *indiscretion*. The word *just* is an exception. The opposite of *just*, meaning "fair, equitable," is *unjust*, but the corresponding noun form is *injustice*. The forms *injust* and *unjustice* are usually not listed in dictionaries and are considered to be misspellings. The corresponding noun for *unjust* is *unjustness*.

inside, inside of *Inside* and *inside of* have the same meaning. *Inside* is generally preferred, especially in writing, when the reference is to position or location: *The materials are inside the warehouse. Inside of* is used more acceptably when the reference is to time: *The 300-page manuscript was photocopied inside of 10 minutes.* A better construction would be *The 300-page manuscript was photocopied in less than 10 minutes.*

insure See **assure, ensure, insure**.

intense, intensive *Intensive* is often used interchangeably with *intense*. However, it refers especially to the strength or concentration of an activity when imposed from without. Thus one speaks of *intense dislike* but *intensive training*.

its, it's *Its*, the possessive form of the pronoun *it*, is never written with an apostrophe. The contraction *it's* (for *it is* or *it has*) is always written with an apostrophe.

joint See **reciprocal, joint**.

kind The use of the plurals *these* and *those* with *kind* (*these kind of films*) has been defended by some as a sensible idiom and attacked by others as ungrammatical and awkward. It is easy enough to substitute *this* (or *that*) *kind of* or *these* (or *those*) *kinds of* but care should be taken that the following nouns and verbs agree in number with *kind*: *This kind of film has had a lot of success in foreign markets. Those are the kinds of books that capture the public imagination.* When *kind of* is used to mean "more or less," it is properly preceded by the indefinite article *a* in formal writing: *The work showed a kind of genius* (not *kind of a genius*). The use of *kind of* to mean "somewhat" (*We were kind of sleepy*) has a casual air to it and should be avoided in formal writing.

kudos *Kudos* means "praise" and is one of those words, like *congeries*, that looks plural but is historically singular. So it is correctly used with a singular verb: *Kudos is due the committee for organizing a successful picnic.*

lack As an intransitive verb meaning "to be deficient," *lack* is used chiefly in the present participle with *in*: *You will not lack in support from the finance committee.* In the sense "to be in need of something," it requires no preposition but is sometimes used with *for*: *You will not lack* (or *lack for*) *support from the graduation committee.* In some cases, however, the two phrasings can convey different meanings: *The millionaire lacks nothing* (has everything). *The millionaire lacks for nothing* (has everything he needs).

latter *Latter*, as used in contrast to *former*, refers to the second of two: *Jones and Smith have been mentioned for transfer to our London office, but the latter may decline the post. Latter* is not appropriate when more than two are named: *Jones, Smith, and Kowalski have been nominated.* Kowalski should then be referred to as *the last, the last named,* or preferably, simply *Kowalski.*

lay, lie *Lay* ("to put, place, or prepare") and *lie* ("to recline or be situated") are frequently confused. *Lay* is a transitive verb and takes an object. *Lay* and its principal parts (*laid, laid, laying*) are correctly used in the following examples: *Please lay the books on the floor. The messenger laid* (not *lay*) *the computer printouts on the desk. The table was laid for four. He was laying the tray down when I came in. Lie* is an intransitive verb and does not take an object. *Lie* and its principal parts (*lay, lain, lying*) are correctly used in the following examples: *The founder of the company often lies* (not *lays*) *down after lunch. When I lay* (not *laid*) *down, I fell asleep. The rubbish had lain* (not *laid*) *in the bin for a week. I was lying* (not *laying*) *in bed when I received the call. The valley lies to the east.* There are a few exceptions to these rules. The idioms *lay low* and *lay for* and the nautical sense of *lay* (*lay at anchor*), though intransitive, are well established.

leave, let In American English *leave* is not an acceptable substitute for *let* in the sense "to allow or permit." Only *let* is acceptable in these examples: *Let me be. Let us not quarrel. Let matters stand.*

lend See **loan, lend.**

less See **fewer, less.**

lie See **lay, lie.**

lighted, lit *Lighted* and *lit* are equally acceptable as past tense and past participle of *light.* Both forms are also well established as adjectives: *The only thing that could be seen in the shuttered room was a lighted* (or *lit*) *candle.*

like There is a traditional injunction against using *like* as a conjunction: *The machine responds as* (not *like*) *it should.* Constructions such as *looks like, sounds like,* and *tastes like* are not objectionable, but *as if* should be substituted in formal writing: *It looks as if there will be no action on the bill before Congress recesses.* There is less objection to the use of *like* when the verb following it is not expressed: *The new senator took to politics like a duck to water.*

likewise   *Likewise* is not a conjunction and cannot take the place of a connective such as *and* or *together with*: *The mayor risked his credibility, likewise his honor.* A better construction would be *The mayor risked his credibility and* (or *and likewise*) *his honor.*

literally   *Literally* means "in a manner that accords precisely with the words." It is often used as if it meant "figuratively" or "in a manner of speaking," which is almost the opposite of its true meaning: *Mary was literally breathing fire.*

loan, lend   Both *lend* and *loan* are acceptable verbs in standard English, although some people hold that *lend* is preferable and that *loan* should be used only as a noun. By this thinking, *lend* is preferred over *loan* in the following examples: *One who lends money to a friend may lose a friend. When I refused to lend my car, I was kicked out of the carpool.* Only *lend* has figurative uses: *All I ask is that you lend an ear to my plea. Some say distance lends enchantment, but others contend that out-of-sight means out-of-mind.*

lot   See **alot.**

majority   When *majority* refers to a particular number of votes, it takes a singular verb: *Her majority was five votes.* When it refers to a group of persons or things that are in the majority, it may take either a plural or singular verb, depending on whether the group is considered as a whole or as a set of individual components. For example, when we refer to an election accomplished by a group as a whole, we say *The majority elects the candidate it wants,* but when we speak of something done individually, such as living within five miles of an office, we say *The majority of our employees live within five miles of the office. Majority* is often preceded by *great* (but not by *greater*) in emphatically expressing the sense "most of": *The great majority has decided not to throw good money after bad.* The phrase *greater majority* is appropriate only when considering two majorities: *A greater majority of the workers has accepted this year's contract than accepted last year's.* Remember that, strictly speaking, *majority* refers to a number greater than 50 percent of the total of a group, what is also called an *absolute majority.* When there are more than two choices in question, as in many elections or surveys, the winner may receive more votes than any other in the group but less than 50 percent of the total. This is called a *plurality*. Sometimes, the word *majority* is used loosely to refer to the largest number in a group, but care should be taken to ensure that readers understand whether a true majority or a plurality is meant.

man Many people consider the word *man* to be sexist when it is used as a synonym for *humankind* or for the generic pronoun *one*. To avoid the implication of sexism, use *man* only when referring to a male person. Gender-neutral substitutes for *man* include *one*, *man or woman*, *human*, and *humanity*.

–*man* compounds Compounds ending in *–man* are considered by many people to be sexist when these words are used to stand for the representative or typical member of groups containing both sexes. A variety of gender-neutral terms have been coined recently as substitutes for compounds ending in *–man*: *police officer*, *firefighter*, *flight attendant*, *letter carrier*, *member of Congress*, *spokesperson*, and so on: *Every citizen* (not *man*) *should have the opportunity to work*. See also **–*person* compounds**.

may See **can**.

means In the sense "financial resources," *means* takes a plural verb: *Our means are more than adequate for this purchase*. In the sense "a way to an end," it may take a singular or plural verb; the choice of a modifier such as *any* or *all* generally determines the number of the verb: *Every means was tried*. *There are several means at our disposal*.

meantime, meanwhile *Meantime* is more common than *meanwhile* as a noun: *In the meantime, we made alternative plans for our vacation*. In expressing the same sense as "in the meantime" as a single adverb, *meanwhile* is more common than *meantime*: *Meanwhile, we made alternative plans for our vacation*.

migrate, emigrate, immigrate *Migrate* is used with reference to both the place of departure and the destination and can be followed by *from* or *to*. It is said of persons, animals, and birds and sometimes implies a lack of permanent settlement, especially as a result of seasonal or periodic movement. *Emigrate* pertains to a single move by a person and implies permanence. It refers specifically to the place of departure and emphasizes movement from that place. If the place is mentioned, the preposition is *from*: *Since many people have emigrated from Russia, we see a new demand for Russian-language books.* *Immigrate* also pertains to a single move by persons and likewise implies permanence; but it refers to destination, emphasizes movement there, and is followed by *to*: *Many people have immigrated to the United States in recent months.*

mitigate, militate The words *mitigate* and *militate* have entirely different meanings but are frequently confused. *Mitigate* means "to moderate the force or intensity of something, alleviate": *New technology can be designed to mitigate the effects of burning fossil fuels. Measures can be taken to mitigate the risks associated with overcrowding in school buildings.* *Mitigate* should not be followed by a preposition such as *against* or *for*. Properly used, *militate* means "to have force or influence" and is often followed by a prepositional phrase starting with *in favor of, for,* or *against*: *The judge finds that the evidence militates in favor of the defendant. The proximity of the ball field to the houses militates against installing lights for night games.*

mobile See **movable, mobile**.

most, mostly The adverb *most* is sometimes used informally in the sense of "almost": *Most all the tapes were on sale last week.* However, this usage should be avoided in formal writing. In the sense "very," as an intensive where no explicit comparison is involved, *most* is acceptable both in writing and in speech: *It proved to be a most ingenious solution.* The adverb *mostly* means "for the greatest part, mainly" or "generally, usually": *The trees are mostly evergreens.* In writing, one should say *for the most part* (not *mostly*) in sentences like *For the most part Northern Telephone is the supplier of our communications equipment.*

movable, mobile Something is *movable* if it can be moved: *All our furniture is movable. There is a movable partition between our desks.* It is *mobile* if it is designed for easy transportation (*The van contained a mobile electric generating unit*) or if it moves frequently (*The company owned several mobile drilling rigs*).

mutual, common *Mutual* is often used to describe a relation between two or more things, and in this use it can be paraphrased with expressions involving *between* or *each other: They met to discuss their mutual relations,* meaning "their relations with each other" or "the relations between them." *Common* describes a relationship shared by the members of a group to something else (*Their common interest is swimming*) or in the expression *common knowledge,* "the knowledge shared by all." The phrase *mutual friend,* however, refers to a friend of each of the several members of a group: *The skating partners were originally introduced by a mutual friend.*

need The verb *need* is used both as a main verb and as an auxiliary verb. As a main verb *need* must agree with its subject and be followed by *to: He needs to find a new job.* As an auxiliary *need* primarily occurs in questions, negations, and *if* clauses. It does not agree with its subject and is not followed by *to: He need not find a new job. Need it be done in a hurry?* The auxiliary *need* means something like "to be obliged to": *You needn't come* (you are under no obligation to come). In this case there is an externally imposed obligation on the subject *you.* If there were no externally imposed obligation, the main verb could be used: *Since I was there when it happened, I don't need to hear* (not *needn't hear*) *the television news account.*

neither *Neither* is construed as singular when it occurs as the subject of a sentence: *Neither of the reports is finished.* Accordingly, a pronoun with *neither* as an antecedent also must be singular: *Neither of the doctors in the lawsuit is likely to reveal his or her identity.* When *neither . . . nor* is used in a conjoined subject, the verb is singular if both nouns are singular (*Neither Damon nor Ed wants to go fishing*), and the verb is plural if both nouns are plural (*Neither the boys nor the girls are interested*). When the construction mixes singular and plural elements, practice is mixed. Many writers place the plural subject second and make the verb plural (*Neither the dog nor the cats have eaten*) or recast the sentence (*The cats haven't eaten, and neither has the dog*).

no When *no* introduces a compound phrase, its elements should be connected with *or* rather than with *nor: James has no experience or interest in coaching hockey. No modification or change in the rules will be acceptable to them.*

nominal   *Nominal* in one of its senses means "in name only." Hence a *nominal payment* is a token payment, bearing no relation to the real value of what is being paid for. The word is often extended in use, especially by sellers, to describe a low or bargain price: *We also acquired an adjacent 600,000-barrel oil reserve at a nominal extra cost.*

no sooner   *No sooner,* as a comparative adverb, should be followed by *than,* not *when: No sooner had I arrived than I had to leave for an emergency meeting. I had no sooner made an offer than they said the property had been sold to another person.*

not   Care should be taken with the placement of *not* and other negatives in a sentence to avoid ambiguity. *All issues are not speculative* could be taken to mean either "All of the issues are not speculative" or "Not all of the issues are speculative." *We didn't sleep until noon* could mean either "We went to sleep at noon" or "We got up before noon."

nothing   *Nothing* takes a singular verb, even when it is followed by a phrase containing a plural noun or pronoun: *Nothing except your fears stands in your path.*

number   As a collective noun *number* may take either a singular or a plural verb. It takes a singular verb when it is preceded by the definite article *the: The number of concert pianists is small.* It takes a plural verb when preceded by the indefinite article *a: A number of the workers are unskilled.*

odd   *Odd,* when used to indicate a few more than a given number, should be preceded by a hyphen to avoid ambiguity: *There are thirty-odd people in line. Odd* in this sense is used only with round numbers.

off   In formal writing, *off* should not be followed by *of* or *from: The speaker stepped off* (not *off of* or *off from*) *the platform.* Nor should *off* be used for *from* to indicate a source in a sentence: *I got a loan from* (not *off*) *the credit union.*

old, older   *Old,* when applied to people, is a blunt term that usually suggests at least a degree of physical infirmity and age-related restrictions. It should be used carefully, especially in referring to people advanced in years but leading active lives. As a comparative form, *older* might logically seem to indicate greater age than *old*, but in most cases the opposite is true. Thus *the older woman in the wool jacket* suggests a somewhat younger person than *the old woman in the wool jacket*. Unlike *elderly*, *older* does not particularly suggest frailness or infirmity, making it the natural choice in many situations.

on, onto, upon   To indicate motion toward a position, both *on* and *onto* can be used: *The dog jumped on (onto) the counter. Onto* is more specific, however, in indicating that the motion was initiated from an outside point, such as from the floor. In constructions where *on* is an adverb attached to a verb, it should not be joined with *to* to form the single word *onto: The lecturer moved on to* (not *onto*) *the next subject*. In their uses to indicate spatial relations, *on* and *upon* are often interchangeable: *The container was resting on* (or *upon*) *the counter*. To indicate a relation between two things, however, instead of between an action and an end point, *upon* cannot always be used: *Hand me the book on* (not *upon*) *the table*.

one   The pronoun *one* is normally singular: *One of the singers has a sore throat*. But the constructions *one or two* and *one or more* take plural verbs: *One or two students from our department have won an award every year. One or more cars were parked on the street during the summer*.

one another   See **each other, one another**.

onetime, one-time   When spelled as a single word, *onetime* means "former." When hyphenated, *one-time* means "only once." Thus a former employee is a *onetime employee*; a mayor who served as mayor only once is a *one-time mayor*.

only   When used as an adverb, *only* should be placed with care to avoid ambiguity. Generally, this means placing *only* next to the word or words that it limits: *Dictators respect only force; they are not moved by words. Dictators only respect force; they do not worship it. She picked up the receiver only when he entered, not before. She only picked up the receiver when he entered; she didn't dial the number*. Occasionally, placement of *only* earlier in the sentence seems more natural: *I can (only) make my decision by Friday of next week only if I receive a copy of the latest report by tomorrow*.

Placement of *only* after *can* would serve the rhetorical function of warning the reader that a condition on the statement follows.

oral See **verbal, oral**.

ought *Ought to* is sometimes used without a following verb if the meaning is clear: *Should we begin soon? Yes, we ought to.* The omission of *to* (*no, we ought not*), however, is not standard. Usages like *one hadn't ought to come* and *one shouldn't ought to say that*, which are common in certain varieties of American English, should be avoided in standard English.

pair *Pair* as a noun can be followed by a singular or plural verb. The singular is always used when *pair* denotes the set taken as a single entity: *This pair of shoes is a year old.* A plural verb is used when the members are considered as individuals: *The pair are working more harmoniously now.*

party A person may be called a *party* in the sense of "participant": *She was a party to the industrial espionage ring. He felt he was the injured party in the dispute.* Except in legal usage, *party* should not be used as a general synonym for *person*: *The person* (not *party*) *who stole $12,000 from the treasury was arrested.*

pass The past tense and past participle of *pass* is *passed*: *They passed* (or *have passed*) *right by the front gate. Past* is the corresponding adjective (*in centuries past*), adverb (*drove past*), and preposition (*past midnight; past the crisis*).

people, persons Traditionally, *people* and *persons* have been distinguished in usage. *People* is the proper term when referring to a large group of individuals, collectively and indefinitely: *People use a wide variety of our products at work and at home. Persons* is applicable to a specific and relatively small number: *Two persons were fired.* In modern usage, however, *people* is also acceptable with any plural number: *I counted two people in the plaza.* The possessive form is *people's* (*the people's rights*) except when *people* is used in the plural to refer to two or more groups considered to be political or cultural entities: *The Slavic peoples' history is marked by tragedy.*

per *Per* is used with reference to statistics and units of measurement: *There is a 10-cent charge per mile. The per-day rate is $125* *per person.* In nontechnical writing, it is preferable to substitute *a* or *each* for *per: A dozen additional dinner guests a* (or *each*) *day was not uncommon.* Its more general use to mean "according to" (*We will work per the terms of this contract, not beyond*) is limited to business and legal writing.

percent, percentage *Percent* is usually written as one word in business material and should be spelled out (that is, instead of using the percent sign) in nontechnical work: *20 percent.* The number of the noun that follows it in a prepositional phrase or that is understood to follow it governs the number of the verb: *Twenty percent of the stock is owned by a conglomerate. Forty-seven percent of our sales come from consumer appliances. Percentage,* when preceded by *the,* takes a singular verb: *The percentage of unskilled workers is small.* When preceded by *a,* it takes either a singular or plural verb, depending on the number of the noun in the prepositional phrase that follows: *A small percentage of the workers are unskilled. A large percentage of the order for that CD was never shipped.*

peremptory See **preemptive, peremptory**.

perfect *Perfect* has been traditionally considered an absolute term, like *unique, chief,* and *prime,* and should not be subject to comparison with *more, less, almost,* and other modifiers of degree. The comparative form nonetheless is used in the United States Constitution in the phrase *a more perfect union.* It is generally regarded as correct when *perfect* is used to mean "ideal for the purposes": *A more perfect spot for our broadcasting station could not be found.*

permit In the sense "to allow for, be consistent with," *permit* is often followed by the preposition *of: The wording of the note permits of several interpretations.* But *of* should not be used when the meaning of permit is "to give permission": *The law permits* (not *permits of*) *camping on the beach.*

–*person* compounds *Person* is increasingly used to create compounds that may refer to either a man or a woman: *chairperson, spokesperson, anchorperson, salesperson.* These forms can be used when the reference is to the position itself, regardless of who might hold it: *The committee should elect a new chairperson at its* *meeting.* They are also appropriate when speaking of the specific individual holding the position: *She was the best anchorperson the local station had ever had.* In cases referring to specific people, alternatives such as *anchorwoman* and *spokesman* are also acceptable and might be preferred by the holder of the position.

persons   See **people, persons.**

personality   *Personality*, meaning "a celebrity" or "a notable," is widely used in speech and journalism; but it should be avoided in this sense in business writing.

persuade   See **convince, persuade**.

phase   See **faze, phase**.

plead   In strict legal usage one is said to *plead guilty* or *plead not guilty* but not to *plead innocent.* In nonlegal contexts, however, *plead innocent* is sometimes used.

plurality   See **majority**.

plus   *Plus* does not have the conjunctive force of *and.* Therefore, when *plus* is used after a singular or plural subject, the verb remains singular: *Two plus two equals four. Inadequate research plus careless writing results in a weak article. Plus* is sometimes used loosely as a conjunction to connect two independent clauses: *We had terrible weather this year, plus our water heater broke.* But this use is not standard and should be avoided in formal contexts.

poor   In formal usage *poor* should be used as an adjective, not an adverb: *Many devote their lives to helping poor people survive.* It should not be used to qualify a verb as in *did poor* or *never worked poorer. Poorly* and *more poorly* are required in such examples.

practical, practicable   *Practical* describes that which is sensible and useful: *They devised a practical approach to the problem. Practicable* means "usable for a specific purpose" and "workable, feasible": *Because your idea is practicable, we may well implement it.* The distinction, however, is often subtle, and many writers use *practical* in both cases. This example illustrates the traditional distinction: *It might be practical to learn some Chinese before going to*

Beijing, but it might not be practicable for someone with a busy schedule and little time to study.

precipitate, precipitant, precipitous The adjective *precipitate* and the adverb *precipitately* often refer to rash, overhasty human actions: *It was a precipitate decision that he soon regretted. Precipitant* and *precipitantly* are also used in the foregoing ways, with stress on rushing forward or falling headlong, literally or figuratively: *The firm was not one to engage in precipitant action. Precipitous* and *precipitously* are used primarily of physical steepness (*a precipitous slope*) or in the figurative extensions of such literal uses (*a precipitous drop in interest rates*).

preemptive, peremptory A *preemptive* action is one that is undertaken to prevent an adversary from acting first: *The preemptive air strike destroyed the enemy's ability to launch an attack. Peremptory* has a range of meanings, including "putting an end to all debate or action" (*The court issued a peremptory decree*); "not allowing contradiction or refusal; imperative" (*The lawyers are entitled to some peremptory challenges dismissing potential jurors*); "having the nature of a command; urgent" (*The teacher spoke in a peremptory tone*); and "offensively self-assured; dictatorial" (*a swaggering, peremptory manner*). Since a *preemptive* military action can be thought of as *peremptory,* the two words are sometimes confused. They should be kept distinct.

prescribe See **proscribe, prescribe.**

presently *Presently* is used primarily in the sense "soon": *Karen will arrive presently.* It is also used in the sense "at the present time": *He is presently (now) living in Chicago.* When you use this word you should make sure that your meaning is clear from the context.

presumptuous, presumptive These two words are related in meaning, but the careful writer should be attuned to their differences. A person who is *presumptuous* presumes too much about someone or a situation and so is overly confident or forward. Thus a remark like *It was highly presumptuous of you to talk like that* is normally intended to accuse someone of being arrogant or inappropriately bold. *Presumptive* was once a synonym of *presumptuous* but now it often describes something that provides a reasonable basis for belief or acceptance: *The presence of so many discarded bills in the room was presumptive evidence that the occupants were engaged in identity theft.* In another use, *presumptive* means "based on presumption or probability, presumed": *The incumbent governor is her party's presumptive nominee for governor in the upcoming election.* This sentence suggests that it is not yet known whether the incumbent governor will receive (or has received) the nomination. Thus, *presumptive* refers to the basis for believing something, and not to forward behavior. Care should be taken to avoid the implication that *presumptuous* was really intended instead of *presumptive* in sentences like *Her presumptive taking over as committee chair has been the occasion of many critical remarks.*

principle, principal *Principal* and *principle* are often confused but have no meanings in common. *Principle* is only a noun and usually refers to a rule or standard: *studying the principles of nuclear physics; refused to compromise his principles.* *Principal* is both a noun and an adjective. As a noun (aside from its specialized meaning in law and finance), it generally denotes a person who holds a high position or plays an important role: *A meeting between all the principals in the transaction had been arranged. She is the new high school principal.* As an adjective it has the related sense of "chief" or "leading": *Only the principal candidates participated in the debate.*

proscribe, prescribe These words have similar sounds but in meaning they are near opposites. The general meaning of *proscribe* is "to forbid or prohibit": *The school's honor system proscribes cheating in any form, including the use of cell phones.* *Prescribe* means "to set down as a rule or guide": *The custom of the time prescribed that the men at the ball should wear frock coats.* The word's most common use is in medicine where it means "to order the use of a medicine or treatment": *The doctor prescribes bed rest and plenty of fluids.*

prove, proved, proven The verb *prove* has two past participles: *proved* and *proven*. While *proved* is the more traditional usage, both are acceptable in standard usage: *The theory has been proved* (or *proven*) *by our mathematicians.* *Proven* is more common as an adjective used directly before a noun: *He is a proven talent. That is a drug of proven effectiveness.*

quick, quickly Both *quick* and *quickly* can be used as adverbs. *Quick* is more frequent in conversation: *Come quick!* In writing the slightly more formal *quickly* is preferred: *When the security guards heard the alarm, they responded quickly.* In the latter example, *quick* would be unacceptable in formal contexts.

quote, cite The verb *quote* is appropriate when words are being given exactly as they were originally written or spoken: *He quoted the first paragraph of the report.* When the reference is less exact, *cite* is preferable: *He cited an advertising study.* The noun *quote* as a substitute for *quotation* has an informal ring to it and should be avoided in formal writing: *The quotation* (not *quote*) *from Milton was the perfect end to her presentation.*

raise, rise *Raise* is properly used as a transitive verb: *Raise the garage door.* For intransitive uses, *rise* is standard: *The elevator rises.* However, *raise* is sometimes used as an intransitive verb: *The window raises easily.* As a noun *raise*, rather than *rise*, is now standard in the United States for an increase in salary, although one still speaks of a *rise in prices.*

rare, scarce *Rare* and *scarce* are sometimes interchangeable, but *scarce* carries an additional implication that the quantities involved are insufficient or inadequate. Thus we speak of *rare books* or of *the rare qualities* of someone we admire but of increasingly *scarce* oil reserves.

rarely, seldom The use of *ever* after *rarely* or *seldom* is considered redundant: *He rarely* (not *rarely ever*) *makes a mistake.* The following constructions, using either *rarely* or *seldom*, are standard, however: *rarely if ever; rarely or never* (not *rarely or ever*).

rather *Rather* is commonly preceded by *would* in expressing preference: *They would rather not eat dinner at home tonight.* *Had* is equally acceptable (*I had rather work nights than be unemployed*), although *had rather* has a decidedly highbrow feel. In a contraction such as *he'd*, either *would* or *had* can be understood: *He'd rather* (*He would* or *had rather*) *be bored than be unemployed.* As a modifier, *rather* is frequently unnecessary and can sound precious: *rather nice; rather cold; rather important.*

reason why See **why.**

reciprocal, joint *Reciprocal*, like *mutual*, can apply to relations between the members of a group, often with reference to an exchange of goods or favors: *They agreed on terms for reciprocal trade. Joint* is often used to describe an undertaking in which several partners are involved: *The joint efforts of federal and local officials will be required to eradicate acid rain.*

refer/reference See **allude/allusion, refer/reference**.

regard, respect *Regard* is usually singular in the phrase *in* (or *with*) *regard to* (not *in regards to*). *Regarding* and *as regards* are also used in the sense "with reference to" but are not as widely acceptable. In the same sense *with respect to* is acceptable, but *respecting* is not. *Respects* is sometimes preferable to *regards* in the sense "particulars": *In some respects* (not *regards*) *you are similar to my friend Robert.*

relatively *Relatively* is always appropriate when a comparison is stated or implied: *The first question was relatively easy* (that is, in comparison to the others). *Relatively* can sound pretentious when used to mean "to some degree, fairly": *I am fairly* (not *relatively*) *sure of it.*

restive, restless *Restive* and *restless* are used as equivalent terms. *Restive*, however, implies more than simply "nervous" or "fidgety." It implies resistance to some sort of restraint. Thus a patient who is sleeping poorly may be *restless*, but the same patient is *restive* only if kept in bed against his or her will.

rise See **raise, rise**.

sacrilegious The adjective *sacrilegious* is often misspelled through confusion with *religious*. It refers to gross irreverence toward something sacred: *His profanity in church was sacrilegious.*

said As an adjective *said* is seldom appropriate to any but legal writing, where it is equivalent to *aforesaid*: *The said tenant* (named in a lease) *agreed to maintain the yard. The said property has a lien on it.* In similar contexts in general usage, *said* should be omitted, as in *the tenant; the property.*

same Only in legal writing is *the same* or *same* used as a substitute for *it* or *them*. In general writing one should be specific: *The* *charge is $5. Please send your payment* (not *Please send the same*) *today.*

scarce See **rare, scarce**.

scarcely *Scarcely* has the force of a negative; therefore, it is not properly used with another negative: *I could scarcely believe it* (not *I couldn't scarcely believe it*). A clause following *scarcely* is introduced by *when* or, less often, by *before* but not by *than*: *The match had scarcely begun when* (or *before*) *it was rained out*.

seasonal, seasonable *Seasonal* and *seasonable*, though closely related, are differentiated in usage. *Seasonal* applies to what depends on or is controlled by the season of the year: *There is always a seasonal increase in unemployment during the late winter months*. *Seasonable* applies to what is appropriate to the season (*seasonable clothing*) or timely (*a seasonable intervention*). Rains are *seasonal* if they occur at a certain time of the year. They are *seasonable* at any time if they save the crops.

seldom See **rarely, seldom**.

semimonthly See **bimonthly, semimonthly**.

set, sit Originally, *set* meant "to cause (something) to sit," so it is now in most cases a transitive verb: *The worker sets his shovel down. One sets the table*. *Sit* is generally an intransitive verb: *They sit at the microphone*. There are some exceptions: *The sun sets* (not *sits*). *A hen sets* (or *sits*) *on her eggs*.

shall, will The traditional rule holds that *shall* is used in the first person to indicate futurity (*I shall leave tomorrow*) and that in the second and third persons the same sense of futurity is expressed by *will* (*He will come this afternoon*). In contemporary American writing *will* is used in all three persons to indicate futurity: *We will be in New York next week*. *Shall* has almost vanished from use as an indicator of future tense, though it is still used in some first-person interrogatives (*Shall we go?*) and in a few set phrases (*We shall overcome*). In formal style and especially in legal documents, Americans use *shall* to express an explicit obligation, as in *Applicants shall provide a proof of residence* and *The Publisher shall provide the Author with an advance*. In general usage, this sense is expressed by *must* or *should*. In writing, a condition other than mere futurity is often expressed more clearly by an alternative to *shall* or *will*, such as *must* or *have to* (indicating determination, compulsion, or obligation) or by use of an intensifying word, such as *certainly* or *surely*: *Participants must register before the race. I will certainly not support that position.*

shine, shone The verb *shine* has two different past tenses, *shined* and *shone*, and these forms also function as past participles. The past tense and past participle *shone* is more frequently used when the verb is intransitive and means "to emit light, be luminous": *The full moon shone brilliantly in the east.* The form *shined*, on the other hand, is used more often when the verb is transitive and means "to direct (a beam of light)" or "to polish" as in *He shined his flashlight down the dark staircase* and *The butler shined the silver.*

should, would Traditionally, the rules governing the use of *should* and *would* were based on the rules governing the use of *shall* and *will*. The rules have been eroded even more in the case of *should* and *would*. Either *should* or *would* is now used in the first person to express conditional futurity: *If I had known that, I should* (or *would*) *have made a different reply.* In the second and third persons, only *would* is acceptable: *If he had known that, he would have made a different reply. Would* cannot always be substituted for *should*, however. *Should* is used in all three persons in a conditional clause: *If I* (or *you* or *he* or *she*) *should decide to go, we will give you a call. Should* is also used in all three persons to express duty or obligation (the equivalent of *ought to*): *I* (or *you* or *he* or *she*) *should go. Would* is used to express volition or promise: *I agreed that I would do it.* Either *would* or *should* is possible as an auxiliary with *like, be inclined, be glad, prefer,* and related verbs: *I would* (or *should*) *like to call your attention to an oversight in the accountant's report.* But *would* is more common than *should. Should have* is sometimes incorrectly written *should of* by writers who have mistaken the source of the spoken contraction *should've.*

since See **as, since.**

sit See **set, sit.**

slow, slowly *Slow* is sometimes used as an informal variant of the adverb *slowly* when it comes after the verb: *We drove the car slow.* But *slowly* should be used in formal contexts. *Slow* is often used informally when brevity and forcefulness are sought: *Drive slow! Slow* is also the established idiomatic form with certain senses of common verbs: *The watch runs slow. Take it slow.*

so The conjunction *so* is followed by *that* when it introduces a clause stating the purpose of or reason for an action: *The supervisor stayed late so that he could catch up on his paperwork. So* can stand alone, however, when it is used to introduce a clause that states the result or consequence of something: *The canning process kills much of the flavor of food, so salt is added.*

so . . . as See **as . . . as, so . . . as.**

stratum The standard singular form is *stratum*; the standard plural is *strata* (or sometimes *stratums*) but not *stratas*.

take See **bring, take.**

tend *Tend* is an informal alternative to *attend* in the phrase *tend to,* meaning "to apply one's attention to": *I stayed home today to tend to (attend to) my garden.*

than, as In comparisons, a pronoun following *than* or *as* may be taken as either the subject or the object of an implied verb whose sense is understood: *John is older than I (am).* The nominative *I* is required since the verb *am* is implied. Yet, in the sentence *It does not surprise me as much as him,* the use of the objective *him* can be justified by analogy to the sentence *It does not surprise me as much as (it surprises) him.*

that, which By the traditional rule, *that* should be used only to introduce a restrictive (or defining) clause, a clause identifying the person or thing being talked about; in this use it should never be preceded by a comma: *The house that Jack built has been torn down.* In this sentence, the clause *that Jack built* is a restrictive clause telling which specific house was torn down. By contrast, *which* should be used only with nonrestrictive (or nondefining) clauses, ones giving additional information about something that has already been identified in the context; in this use, *which* is always preceded by a comma. Thus one should say *The students in Chemistry 101 have been complaining about the textbook, which* (not *that*) *is hard to follow.* The clause *which is hard to follow* is nonrestrictive in that it does not indicate which text is being complained about; even if it were omitted, we would know that the phrase *the textbook* refers to the text in Chemistry 101. It should be easy to follow the rule in nonrestrictive clauses like this, since *which* here sounds more natural than *that.*

Some people extend the rule and insist that, just as *that* should be used only in restrictive clauses, *which* should be used only in nonrestrictive clauses. By this thinking, *which* should be avoided in sentences such as *I need a book which will tell me all about city gardening.* In this sentence the restrictive clause *which will tell me all about city gardening* describes what sort of book is needed. But this use of *which* with restrictive clauses is very common, even in edited prose. Moreover, in some situations *which* is preferable to *that. Which* can be especially useful where two or more relative clauses are joined by *and* or *or: It is a philosophy in which ordinary people may find solace and which many have found reason to praise. Which* may also be preferable when introducing a restrictive clause modifying a preceding phrase that contains *that: We want to assign only that material which will be most helpful.* See also **which**.

this, that   *This* and *that* are both used as demonstrative pronouns to refer to a thought expressed earlier: *The door was unopened; that* (or *this*) *in itself casts doubt on the guard's theory. That* is sometimes prescribed as the better choice in referring to what has gone before (as in the preceding example). When the referent is yet to be mentioned, only *this* is used: *This is what bothers me—we have no time to consider late applications.* When used as an adjective, *this* often occurs in speech as an emphatic variant of the indefinite article *a: This friend of mine is moving to Portland. I have this terrible headache.* But this usage is casual and should be avoided in formal writing.

tight   *Tight* as an adverb appears after the verb when it follows verbs such as *squeeze, shut, close, tie,* and *hold: The father told the child to hold on tight to the railing. Close it tight.* In most cases the adverb *tightly* also may be used in this position: *Close it tightly.* In a few cases *tight* is the only form that may be used: *They told us to sit tight and not to worry. Sleep tight, little one.* Before a verb only *tightly* is used: *The money supply will be tightly controlled.*

together with *Together with*, like *in addition to*, is often employed following the subject of a sentence or clause to introduce an addition. The addition, however, does not alter the number of the verb, which is governed by the subject: *The chairperson* (singular), *together with two aides, is expected in an hour.* The same is true of *along with, as well as, besides,* and *in addition to*: *Common sense as well as training is a requisite for the job.*

too *Too* preceded by *not* or another negative is frequently used informally as a form of understatement to convey humor or sarcasm: *The workers were not too pleased with the amount of their raises. This comedian is not too funny. Not too,* when used to mean approximately "not very," is also considered casual: *Passage of the bill is not now considered too likely.* Such casual use should be avoided in more formal writing. *Too* can often be eliminated from such sentences without loss; but if deletion gives undue stress to the negative sense, the writer may find *not very* or *none too* preferable choices: *The comedian is not very funny. Too* is often used in writing in place of *moreover* or *in addition* to introduce a sentence: *There has been a cutback in oil production; too, rates have been increasing.* This usage also should be avoided in formal situations.

torn *Torn*, never *tore*, is the standard past participle of the verb *tear*: *I have torn a page of the book.*

tortuous, torturous, tortured Although *tortuous* and *torturous* have a common Latin source, their primary meanings are distinct. *Tortuous* means "twisting" (*a tortuous road*) or by extension "extremely strained or devious" (*tortuous reasoning*). *Torturous* and *tortured* refer primarily to *torture*. However, these words can also be used in the sense of "twisted," "strained," or "belabored": *a tortured analogy*.

transpire *Transpire* has long been used in the sense "to become known": *It soon transpired that they intended to vote for my opponent.* The meaning "to happen" or "to take place" has come into use more recently: *Marcia wondered what would transpire next.* This latter use is often considered pretentious or pompous.

try and, try to *Try and* is common in informal conversation for *try to*, especially in established combinations such as *try and* *stop me* and *try and get some rest*. In most contexts, however, it is not interchangeable with *try to* unless the situation is clearly informal. The following is unacceptable in formal writing: *It is a mistake to try and force compliance with a rule that is so unpopular.*

type   *Type* is followed by *of* in constructions like *that type of leather*. The variant form that omits *of*, as in *that type leather*, is generally considered nonstandard. See also **kind**.

under way   See **way, under way, aweigh**.

unexceptional, unexceptionable   *Unexceptional* is often confused with *unexceptionable*. When the desired meaning is "not open to objection" or "above reproach," the term is *unexceptionable*: *She presented unexceptionable arguments for her curious behavior on the train. Unexceptional* should be used to mean "not exceptional," that is, "not varying from the usual": *Although the course sounded like it would be complex and interesting, it proved to be unexceptional.*

uninterested   See **disinterested, uninterested**.

upon   See **on, onto, upon**.

used to   The verb *use* is used in the past tense with an infinitive to indicate a past condition or habitual practice: *We used to live in that house.* Because the *–d* in *used* has merged with the *t* of *to* and is not pronounced in these constructions, people sometimes mistakenly leave it out when writing. Thus it is incorrect to write *We use to play tennis.* When *do* occurs with this form of use in negative statements and in questions, the situation is reversed, and *use to* (not *used to*) is correct: *Mr. Jones did not use to worry so much. Didn't she use to work for your company?*

various   *Various*, sometimes appearing as a collective noun followed by *of*, is not standard usage: *He spoke to various of the members.* It is correct as an adjective in the sense "of diverse kinds": *She left early for various reasons.*

venal, venial   The words *venal* and *venial* look and sound similar but have very different meanings. In general, *venal* refers to monetary corruption. A venal police officer is one who is given or susceptible to bribery or is otherwise capable of betraying scruples for a price. *Venial*, from the Latin *venia*, "forgiveness," means "easily excused or forgiven," as in *a venial offense*. *Venial* is most often found in the phrase *venial sin*, which is sometimes extended to nonreligious contexts. In Catholic theology, a venial sin is one that is minor and that does not incur damnation. It stands in contrast to mortal sin.

verbal, oral   In the sense "by word of mouth," *verbal* is synonymous with *oral*. In other senses *verbal* has to do with words either written or spoken, such as verbal communication (as opposed to communication through gestures or body language). *Verbal*, when applied to terms such as *agreement, promise, commitment,* and *understanding,* is well established as a synonym of *oral*. But anyone who fears misunderstanding may use *oral* instead: *They struck an oral* (or *verbal*) *agreement*.

–ward, –wards   Since the suffix *–ward* indicates direction, there is no need to use *to the* with it: *The cargo ship is sailing westward* (or *to the west*).

way, under way, aweigh   *Way,* not *ways,* is the generally accepted form in writing when the term refers to distance: *We have a long way to go.* The phrase *under way* (meaning "in motion" or "in progress") is written as two words or as one (*underway*), including reference to the nautical (*underway* not *under weigh*). Confusion sometimes arises because an anchor is *weighed* and, when off the bottom, is *aweigh*.

well   See **good, well**.

whatever   *Whatever* (pronoun) and *what ever* are used in questions and statements: *Whatever* (or *what ever*) *made them say that?* Both forms are used, although the one-word form is more common. (The same is true of *whoever, whenever, wherever,* and *however* when used in corresponding senses.) For the adjective only the one-word form is used: *Take whatever office supplies you need.* When the phrase preceding a restrictive clause is introduced by *whatever, that* should not be used: *Whatever book that you want to look at will be sent to your office.* A more elegant construction would be *Whatever book you want to look at will be sent to your office.*

when   In informal speech *when* is often used after the verb *be* in definitions: *A dilemma is when you don't know which way to turn.* This usage, however, is widely regarded as incorrect or unsuitable to formal discourse. Avoiding *when* in these sentences is tricky and requires making the first part of the sentence a full clause: *A dilemma is a situation in which you don't know which way to turn. You are in a dilemma when you don't know which way to turn.*

where   When *where* refers to "the place from which," it requires the preposition *from*: *Where did you come from?* When it refers to "the place to which," it requires no preposition: *Where did they go (to)?* When *where* refers to "the place at which," it also requires no preposition: *Where are they (at)?*

which   *Which* sometimes refers to an entire preceding statement rather than to a single word: *The drilling failed to turn up any new oil reserves, which disturbed the geologist.* In this acceptable example the reference is clear. But when *which* follows a noun, the antecedent may be in doubt and ambiguity may result: *The inspector filed the complaint, which was a surprise.* If *which* is intended to refer to the entire first clause rather than to the complaint, the desired sense would be expressed more clearly by this construction: *We learned that the inspector had filed the complaint, and that discovery came as a surprise to us.* See also **that, which**.

whose   *Whose*, as the possessive form of a relative pronoun, can refer to both persons and things. Thus it functions as the possessive of both *who* and *which*. The following example, in which *whose* refers to an inanimate object, is acceptable: *The car, whose design is ultramodern, is typical of the new styles.* (The alternative possessive form of *which* is also used in referring to things but is sometimes cumbersome in application.)

why   *Why* is redundant in *the reason why*: *The reason (why) they joined the new health club is not clear.* The sentence could also be recast: *Their reasons for joining the new health club are not clear.*

will   See **shall, will**.

–wise   The suffix *–wise* has long been used to mean "in the manner or direction of": *clockwise, likewise, otherwise,* and *slantwise.* It is particularly overused as business jargon meaning "with relation to" and attachable to any noun such as *saleswise* and *inflationwise*. Generally considered inelegant, the *–wise* suffix should be used with caution: *The report is not encouraging saleswise. Taxwise, however, it is an attractive arrangement.* It is easy enough to rephrase such sentences: *The report is not encouraging in terms of potential sales. For tax savings, it is an attractive arrangement.*

with *With* does not have the conjunctive force of *and*. Consequently, in the following example the verb is governed by the singular subject and remains singular: *The superintendent, with his assistant, is expected at the science fair on Monday.*

would See **should, would**.

wreak *Wreak* is sometimes confused with *wreck*, perhaps because the *wreaking* of damage may leave a *wreck: The storm wreaked havoc along the coast.* The past tense and past participle of *wreak* is *wreaked*, not *wrought*, which is an alternative past tense and past participle of *work* that usually sounds old-fashioned.

A GUIDE TO
Writing

A resumé, sometimes called a *curriculum vitae*, or *CV* for short, is a concise description of your qualifications for a job, including a history of your work experience and schooling. Your resumé should be used to make your skills and abilities known to a prospective employer. In many cases, your resumé is all you have to convince an employer that it is worth spending the time and money to interview you. Even if a resumé is not normally required to apply for the kind of job you are seeking, a carefully composed resumé can set you apart from other candidates.

Since you will have limited space on which to present everything relevant about your work history, you must be concise, well organized, and clear in your presentation and format. An employer may have to look through a hundred or more resumés for the same job before selecting people to be interviewed. Therefore, your resumé must be written so that someone scanning it can immediately pick out your best assets and work experience.

Preparation

The first step is to take an inventory of your present abilities and the responsibilities you've had in your present and previous positions, and put them into categories similar to the ones in the following list: *planning and organization, project coordination and management, writing and editing, supervision, training, purchasing, record keeping, word processing.*

If you intend to change careers, try making your categories more general to see how your skills might apply to a different kind of work.

Once you have assessed your own skills, find out which skills employers in your industry are looking for so that you can emphasize these aspects on your resumé. It is important to tailor your resumé to your audience. If you are submitting your resumé to a particular company as opposed to just posting it online, it should show that you have researched that company and understand their business. Make sure you at least visit the company's website and read the job description carefully.

Check the Internet for e-resumé preparation and submission

tips, including resumé banks such as Monster.com where you can post your resumé, and make note of available writing services in case you need help in preparation. Various sites explain the formatting requirements and the various steps you should follow in sending your resumé by e-mail, in posting it directly to a resumé databank on an e-form, or in submitting a scannable paper resumé (follow the instructions precisely).

The resumé sites also have a wealth of other information, such as how to do an online job search, how to find job networking opportunities, and how to create a webpage advertising your skills and services to prospective employers. Many sites also have sample resumés and cover letters along with writing tips.

Although e-resumés have certain advantages (for example, they show an employer that you know how to use such technologies), it's important to be aware of the pitfalls too. Assess the resumé banks you're considering, and choose those that selectively target employers instead of broadcasting resumés.

Also, be aware that your current employer may discover your resumé on a job-seekers' site. Some agencies unethically take resumés from a site and post them elsewhere. To avoid this, include a statement when you file your resumé saying that it may not be posted elsewhere by others. As a further precaution, file your resumé *without your name*. Instead, have replies sent to an anonymous e-mail account. Or don't post your resumé at all; rather, register with an online job agent service that will e-mail appropriate want ads directly to you.

Format

The general format that you use for a resumé depends in part on the information you want to emphasize and the type of job you're seeking. It also depends on whether you intend to submit it as a traditional paper resumé, a scannable paper resumé, an e-mail attachment, or an e-form resumé to be posted in a job databank. If you send an electronic version, you should ask the recipients in your accompanying e-mail message if they would like a printed copy for their records.

Unless you're having your resumé prepared by a resumé writing service, you should not only check the information available on the Internet but also review a current book on resumés and cover letters. Books explaining how to use the Internet for job searches are also available.

The appearance of your resumé is almost as important as its content, because it's a reflection of your professionalism. To project a professional, businesslike image, follow these general guidelines:

- Use quality, 20-pound, white or off-white paper for copies submitted by traditional mail.
- Use a high-quality copying process.
- Don't include personal information other than your name, residence/mailing address, telephone and fax numbers, and e-mail address. Employers don't need to know your marital status, height, weight, or sex and can't legally require you to provide extensive personal data. As a general rule, your resumé should not include any information that is not directly related to your ability to perform the responsibilities of the job you are applying for.
- Include a heading (name, address, telephone and fax numbers, e-mail address, website) followed by your job objective (optional), work experience, educational background, and any pertinent information you want to list about other matters, such as skills or awards.
- Use action words (*developed, managed,* and so on) and the active voice (*I did,* not *it was done*), and avoid illogical changes in verb tenses (*arrange/arranged*) throughout the resumé.
- Emphasize nouns (*telecommunications, records management,* and so on) in your resumé since some employers use computers to scan resumés for keywords that match their job requirements.
- Try to keep the format open, uncluttered, and easy to read, and avoid overuse of all-capital letters or italic type.
- Spell out names of organizations and titles.
- List educational and work experience in reverse order (most recent first).
- Use different headings for different categories of work or activities, such as *Student Teaching Experience, Community Volunteer Work,* and *Special Skills.*

- Be truthful, and don't overstate your skills or experience or provide other inaccurate or misleading information.
- Spell-check and manually proofread your resumé carefully, several times, and have someone else also proofread it a final time.

A resumé that emphasizes previous types and places of employment is sometimes called a *chronological resumé*. This common format is easy to follow and focuses on your job history and career development. However, if you want to emphasize your skills and abilities instead, you may want to use a *functional resumé*. This type of resumé details your skills and abilities under the specific function areas that you choose to highlight. If you've had too few or too many jobs, or if your experience looks scattered, a functional resumé is desirable because it focuses on your marketable skills and avoids giving the impression that you haven't been around enough or have made too many moves.

Parts of the resumé

Objectives. Many people choose to begin their resumé with a brief paragraph that may be labeled "Objectives." In this paragraph, you indicate what job you are looking for (this should always be the job you are applying for) and your major qualifications for such a job. Or you may simply use this paragraph to state your basic strengths and the nature of your past work. Be careful about stating a specific job title, such as "executive assistant"— you could be limiting your opportunities. There may be another job available that can combine all your skills with a title that doesn't even resemble "executive assistant."

Work experience. The record of your work experience should begin with your most recent job. Usually, you give the title you held for each job, the name of the company (and division when relevant), its location, and your dates of employment. If you do not want to reveal the name of your current employer in your resumé, then you may replace it with a descriptive phrase, such as "independent engineering consulting firm."

The descriptions of your previous jobs should be short

summaries of your responsibilities, accomplishments, and contributions to the positions. Tailor your descriptions to the position you are applying for by highlighting the most relevant aspects of your work experience. In addition, emphasize favorable patterns or trends, such as a series of promotions to jobs of increased responsibility. Remember to use active verbs and short sentences.

Though resumés are generally kept to one page, if you have worked for a long time at a variety of different jobs, it may be necessary to use two pages.

Education. Unless you are applying for your first job, your record of your education should follow your work history, beginning with the school or training program you attended most recently. Include the name of the institution, the dates you were registered as a student, and any degrees or certificates you received. If you have attended college, it is not necessary to list your high school or grade school.

Skills and activities. The rest of your resumé should present relevant activities, skills, or accomplishments that do not fit into the other sections. These may include hobbies, affiliations, your schooling, degrees, honors, publications, patents, proficiency in languages, or computer skills. If you belong to professional societies, you should definitely list them. If you belong to social, civic, or volunteer organizations, list them only if you believe your membership in them is an asset. List any important awards or honors you have received whether or not they are job-related. All decisions about what to include should be made from the perspective of your potential employer.

Looking for your first job

If you are looking for your first full-time job, you must compose your resumé somewhat differently. Since you have not had any substantial work experience, your school record is the primary indication of your ability and seriousness of purpose.

Under each academic institution list any courses you took or projects you worked on that demonstrate your qualifications for the job. Extracurricular activities, such as sports or clubs, can be listed here as well or placed in a separate section at the bottom of the page. If you have not graduated yet, give the date you expect to graduate along with the degree and major you are studying for. Many employers also look for cumulative grade point averages (GPA) and standardized test scores. If your GPA within your major is higher than your overall GPA, you should include both (especially if your major is relevant to the job).

Your work history should include any part-time jobs, summer jobs, or volunteer jobs you have held, even if they are unrelated to the type of work you are seeking. In your descriptions, emphasize your reliability, leadership, and organizational skills.

In any resumé that you prepare, you should be sure to account for all time between the end of schooling and the present. If you have taken off a year and traveled, say so. If you have attempted unsuccessfully to start your own business, say so. It is far better to state what you have been involved in than to allow a prospective employer to wonder what you have been doing with your time.

Sample resumés. On the following pages are two sample resumés. The first is for a person looking for a first job. The second is for a person who has already held two jobs.

Cover letter

When you write to a prospective employer, you should always send a cover letter with your resumé or an e-mail with your resumé attachment (unless an ad to which you're replying asks you not to do this). Your message should be brief and businesslike while sparking the interest of the prospective employer. It should convey that you've researched the company and have related your skills to the company's needs, but it should not be a repetition of all the information contained in the resumé. You should state the specific position you are interested in, briefly discuss your experience, and refer the reader to the enclosed resumé. At the end of the letter you may wish to indicate that you will telephone the prospective employer for an interview. Since your letter may be scanned by computer, along with your resumé, it's important to use keywords (nouns), as described previously.

You will, of course, have to write a separate cover letter for

BARBARA L. FENTON
123 Lucinda Avenue • Upland, CA 91786
E-mail: fentonb@wsu.edu • Phone: 555.765.4321

EDUCATION

Sept. 2002–present Claremont, CA	**WESTERN STATE UNIVERSITY** *Finance Major* • Expected to graduate May 2006. • GPA: 3.2 cumulative, 3.6 in department. • Relevant courses: International Economics, Money and Banking, Econometrics, Developing Economies, Russian Economic History, Financial Markets, Calculus, Statistics and Data Analysis. • Wrote thesis on competition among landscaping firms in Southern California. **EXTRACURRICULAR ACTIVITIES** • Presently volunteering five hours a week for the Big Brothers Big Sisters program. • Organized the university's first intramural basketball league. • Managed annual intramural basketball tournament.

EXPERIENCE

Academic Year 2004, Academic Year 2005 Claremont, CA	**CAPTAIN'S COVE RESTAURANT** *Server* • Promoted to head server after only three months. • Responsible for closing restaurant twice a week. • Recognized for regular attendance.
Summer 2004, Summer 2005 Upland, CA	**UPLAND CHAMBER OF COMMERCE** *Summer Intern* • Designed a spreadsheet to manage membership records and streamline quarterly mailings. • Prepared a presentation forecasting the economic impact of a local housing development.
Summer 2002, Summer 2003 Upland, CA	**GREEN LAWN LANDSCAPING** *Landscaper* • Improved the company's method of installing sprinklers after attending a voluntary training course. • Introduced practice of salvaging leftover materials to reduce costs.

COMPUTER SKILLS

	• Excel, Microsoft Office, Bloomberg, LexisNexis

Resumé for Entry-Level Applicant

each specific position you want to apply for. The cover letter, like the resumé, should be neat and should be printed on quality paper. Remember that the cover letter serves as your introduction to a prospective employer and that first impressions are very

MATTHEW ARBIZU

123 Lincoln Street   Richmond, Virginia 23226
E-mail: mattarbizu@freenet.com   *Phone:* 555.765.4321

OBJECTIVE
To find a job that would utilize a broad range of my managerial and business skills and would offer the potential for advancement in a large company.

EXPERIENCE

2002–present
Richmond, VA

BIGPHARMA, INC.
Executive Secretary to Vice President, Human Resources
- Managed all office activities in vice president's absence.
- Upgraded computer systems and led project to digitize all archived records.
- Scheduled executive committee meetings and recorded minutes for distribution to committee members.
- Responsible for disseminating confidential personnel information to regional branch offices.
- Supervised five full-time assistants and temporary help.
- Prepared and scheduled newspaper and Internet ads for corporate job openings.

1997–2002
Virginia Beach, VA

DUNN AND TAYLOR ADVERTISING, INC.
Account Secretary
- Organized and maintained electronic and paper client files for three executives.
- Scheduled layout, design, and launch meetings with freelance designers and staff writers.
- Corresponded with clients about scheduled advertising activity.
- Arranged travel and itineraries for account executives.

EDUCATION

1999–2002
Virginia Beach, VA

BUSINESS INSTITUTE
Master of Business Administration

1996
Hampton Roads, VA

EASTERN STATE UNIVERSITY
Bachelor of Arts in Communications

SKILLS

COMPUTERS
HTML, Microsoft Office, Lotus Notes

LANGUAGES
English, Spanish, Arabic

Resumé for Experienced Applicant

important. Be sure that the spelling and grammar are correct and that you have spelled all names and addresses properly.

If you are sending a resumé via e-mail, your cover letter should appear in the text of the e-mail, with the resumé document attached. Just as with a printed letter, be absolutely sure that the e-mail is error-free. Remember that your e-mail address contributes to a prospective employer's impression of you as well, and be sure that it is professional and respectful.

Refer to the following sample cover letter and also study the models of winning cover letters provided on the Internet and in published resumé books. Consider having the letter, as well as

---

100 School Street
Framingham, MA 01701
508-555-0505

February 11, 20‒‒

Ms. Valerie Kaishian
Human Resources Manager
Trademark Publications
50 Broad Street
Boston, MA 02110

Dear Ms. Kaishian:

I'd like to apply for the position of editorial assistant advertised in the February 10 edition of the *Boston Globe*. I believe this position would give me an excellent opportunity to apply my six years of experience in publishing and to use my strong educational background in English and written communication. My resumé is enclosed for your review.

I greatly enjoyed my work in the editorial departments of two other publishing companies. In addition to handling the manuscript-review process, I communicated regularly with outside authors concerning deadlines and production schedules.

It would be a challenge and a privilege to work with the writers and editors at Trademark Publications, a company well known for its quality books and journals, and I'd like to tell you about my qualifications and how they match your requirements. I look forward to hearing from you about the possibility of a personal interview.

Thank you very much, Ms. Kaishian.

Sincerely,

Elizabeth Simms

Enc.: Resumé

Cover Letter for Resumé

your resumé, prepared by a professional resumé-writing service if you have any doubts about your skill in doing it yourself.

Interview follow-up letter

Always send a follow-up thank-you letter to your interviewer. This professional courtesy may be the touch that gets you the job over another equally qualified applicant. Following is an example of a brief but thoughtful message.

---

100 School Street
Framingham, MA 01701
508-555-0505

February 27, 20—

Mr. Lee C. Costa
Editorial Director
Trademark Publications
50 Broad Street
Boston, MA 02110

Dear Mr. Costa:

EDITORIAL ASSISTANT POSITION

Thank you for the opportunity to discuss the editorial assistant position at Trademark Publications. I'm very excited about the work that you described during my interview yesterday. It sounds challenging, and I know that the activities involved in the position would motivate me to pursue an editorial career with great enthusiasm.

I want to reiterate my strong interest in the position, and I also want to thank you for taking time to show me around the company and explain in detail the nature of its publications. I look forward to further discussions with you.

Thank you very much, Mr. Costa.

Sincerely,

Elizabeth Simms

Follow-Up Thank-You Letter

Letter formats

For traditional, hard-copy letters, the three most common business formats are the full-block, modified-block, and simplified-block formats. A personal style, used on smaller-size, personal (non-company) stationery, is appropriate for certain personal or social business letters, such as a thank-you note for a gift or a sympathy message to a coworker or customer. This type of letter may be prepared in either a full-block or modified-block style, according to preference. Some people also use a variation of one of the three standard formats or a combination of two or more formats.

The models on the following pages (Full-Block Format, Modified-Block Format, and Simplified-Block Format) indicate their principal differences and format specifications, such as the proper line spacing to use between elements.

Major parts of a letter

The major parts of a traditional business letter—usually presented in the following order—are the date, confidential notation, inside address, attention line, salutation, subject, body, complimentary close, signature, reference initials, filename notation, enclosure notation, delivery notation, copy notation, postscript, and continuation page heading. These elements must be properly arranged on the page with ample margins (usually a minimum of 1 inch top and bottom and about $1^1/_2$ inches on both sides).

Date. The date includes the month, day, and year: *September 4, 2006.* In military style, the day is placed before the month and no comma is used: *4 September 2006.* All numerals *(9/4/06)* should be avoided since people may not read the numbers in the same way. In some countries, for example, *9/4/06* would be read as *April 9, 2006,* rather than *September 4, 2006.*

Place the date two or more lines below the last line of the letterhead, flush left in the full-block and simplified-block formats and at the page center or slightly right of it in the modified-block format.

February 4, 20--

Mr. William C. Cross
ABC Chemicals Ltd.
321 Park Avenue East
City, ST 98765

Dear Mr. Cross:

FULL-BLOCK LETTER FORMAT

This is a full-block letter format, featuring all elements aligned with the left margin.

The date is placed two or more lines below the letterhead, and the inside address begins three or more lines below the date. The salutation appears two lines below the inside address and the subject two lines below the salutation. The body begins two lines below the subject. The complimentary close is placed two lines below the last line of the message body, and the printed signature is about four lines beneath it.

Concluding notations may be single- or double-spaced, depending on available space.

Sincerely,

John M. Swanson
Executive Vice President

rs

Encs.: 4

cross.ltr

Full-Block Format

Confidential notation. Use a confidential, or personal, notation on a letter and envelope when you don't want anyone other than the addressee to open the letter. Place the word *Confidential* or *Personal* in all capital letters or with an initial capital two to

1-PAGE FAX TO 800-555-6543

February 4, 20—

Dr. David J. Peters
State Insurance Corporation
4556 Hightower Boulevard
City, ST 98765

Dear Dr. Peters:

MODIFIED-BLOCK LETTER FORMAT

This is a modified-block letter format, which is a more traditional style than the full-block format. The date, complimentary close, and signature block are all aligned at or just past the center of the page.

A fax notation may be placed at the top of the letter or with the other end-of-letter notations. When the fax notation is placed at the top, the date begins two lines below it. The inside address and salutation are flush with the left margin, as they would be in a full-block format. The subject and paragraphs, however, are indented.

Otherwise, the spacing is the same as that used in the full-block format. Concluding notations may be single- or double-spaced.

Cordially,

Donna W. Reardon
Human Resources Manager

Enc.: Brochure

cc: Jim Hartley

Modified-Block Format

four lines below the date (and also on the envelope below the return address):

January 4, 20—

CONFIDENTIAL

COMPANY LETTERHEAD

February 4, 20—

Ms. Barbara C. Mackie
HCI Corporation
One State Street
City, ST 98765

SIMPLIFIED-BLOCK LETTER FORMAT

Ms. Mackie, this is a model of the simplified format. It's a clean, modern
style designed for easy formatting and composition.

The date is flush with the left margin two or more lines beneath the letterhead. The inside address, also flush left, is two or more lines below the date.
The salutation is omitted in this format, but the addressee's name is often
mentioned in the first and last paragraphs to personalize the letter.

The subject is placed three lines below the inside address, and the message
begins three lines after that. Since there's no complimentary close, Ms.
Mackie, the signature is placed about five lines below the message. The traditional concluding notations are handled the same as in other formats.

Jane M. Wright
Senior Editor

By UPS Next-Day Air

P.S. You may enjoy reading the enclosed booklet about formatting letter
reports. JMW

Simplified-Block Format

Inside address. Place the inside address flush left, regardless of
the letter format, three or more lines below the date, depending
on the length of the letter. Include all data necessary for correct
identification and delivery of the letter. This may include the
recipient's name; job title; company name; department; street

address; suite or other number; and city, state, and Zip Code, as well as the country in the case of international mail. (See also *Attention Line*.)

Use a personal or professional title before the addressee's name: *Mr., Ms., Dr., Professor,* or other title. (Since *Ms.* is not used in other countries, use the country's equivalent of *Miss* or *Mrs.*) If you don't know if a person is a man or a woman, omit the title: *A. J. Wilson.* Place scholastic abbreviations, such as *PhD,* after the name. If a person has more than one degree, place the one pertaining to the person's profession first. (See *Forms of Address* for more about the use of personal and professional titles.) Spell out all numerical street names through ten (*14 Tenth Avenue*), but use figures for house and building numbers, except the number one (*One McKenzie Street*), and separate a house or building number from a street number with a hyphen (*2 – 17 Street*). Room and suite numbers should be on the same line as the street address:

> Dr. Dolores Acosta, President
> CCC Corporation
> 1234 Matthews Street, Suite 4
> City, ST 98765

> Mr. J. H. Parsons, Vice President, Sales
> CCC Corporation Ltd.
> Research and Development Division
> One Boyleston Avenue, Room 10
> Ottawa, ON K1A OB1
> CANADA

Attention line. Address your letter to the company, and use an attention line on both the envelope and the letter when you want to be certain that someone else will open and read the letter if the person named in the attention line is absent. You may also address a letter to one person and name another in the attention line. Then if the addressee is absent, the person named in the attention line will open the letter.

Position the attention line flush left within the inside address—on the first line if the letter is addressed generally to a firm or after the addressee's name if the letter is addressed to a person. Spell out the word *Attention,* and use the person's full name without a title:

Attention Ellen Rivera
ABC Incorporated
567 Tower Court
City, ST 98765

Mr. John Grayson
Attention Rana Farhan
ABC Incorporated
567 Tower Court
City, ST 98765

Salutation. Place the salutation, or greeting, two lines below the inside address, flush left in the full-block and modified-block formats. Omit the salutation in the simplified-block format. Capitalize the word *Dear* and the words of a formal title such as *Your Excellency*, and place a colon after the last word.

In letters addressed to a company or department, with or without an attention line, use a general greeting, such as *Ladies and Gentlemen* or *Dear Members of the Sales Department,* but not *Dear ABC Incorporated* or *Dear Sales Department.* Use first names only when you're certain a recipient wants to be addressed that way. Use first names in international correspondence only when the recipient has specifically asked to be addressed that way. Refer to *Forms of Address,* beginning on page 157, for information on the use of personal and professional titles in salutations:

Dear Ms. Smith:
Dear Ms. Kline and Mr. Jackson:
Dear Dr. Fuentes and Ms. Adams:
Dear Mss. Wehbe, Thomas, and Osmon:
Dear Dr. Browne, Ms. Hendricks, and Mr. Rider:
Dear Jan:
Dear Jan and Karim:
Dear A. B. Renfro: (*gender unknown*)
Dear Professor Lee:
Dear Major Benson:
Dear Señora Gonzalez: (*letter to other country*)
Ladies and Gentlemen: (*letter to company*)
Dear Sales Manager: (*name unknown*)
Dear Sir: (*very formal*)
Dear Madam: (*very formal*)
Most Reverend Sir: (*very formal*)

To Whom It May Concern: (*letter to unknown recipients*)
Dear Friends: (*letter to group of people*)

Subject. A subject summarizes the main topic of a message and makes it unnecessary for the writer to announce the subject in the first paragraph. Place the subject flush left, two lines below the salutation in the full-block format and three lines below the salutation in the simplified-block format. Place it two lines below the salutation and indent it the same as the paragraphs in the modified-block format.

Often the word *Subject* is omitted. If it's used, however, put a colon after it, and write it and the words that follow in all capital letters or capitalize each important word, as preferred. (Law offices commonly use the words *In re* or *Re,* with no colon after them, rather than the word *Subject.* In this case, the line should be placed *above,* rather than after, the salutation.) If possible, use a single subject and focus on that one main topic in the letter:

> NOVEMBER SALES MEETING
> SUBJECT: NOVEMBER SALES MEETING
> SUBJECT: November Sales Meeting
> Subject: November Sales Meeting

Body. Single-space the body, or the discussion part of the message, and leave one blank line between the paragraphs. Begin the body two lines below the subject or the salutation in the full-block and modified-block formats and three lines below the subject in the simplified-block format. Place paragraphs flush left in the full block and simplified-block formats, and indent them about half an inch in the modified block format.

Business reports prepared as letters may have subheads and other features, such as lists. If headings are used, place them flush left or centered, with one or more blank lines above and below each head, or position them run in with the first line of a paragraph. Write the headings in all capitals, with important words capitalized, or with an initial capital only, as preferred, and print them in a larger size or in an italic or bold face, if desired. Although they should be distinctive, it's usually best to avoid distracting design flairs and flourishes in business correspondence.

Lists in a letter should be set off from the rest of the body, usually with one blank line before and after the list and sometimes with a space between each list item. A list may also be indented from the left (or from both the left and right) as a block, using the same amount of indention as that used for any paragraph, often about half an inch. Single-space the items in a list, the same as the rest of the message.

Quotations in a letter that exceed four or five lines should be set off from the rest of the body as a blocked quotation, or extract. An extract is usually indented the same as a paragraph, or about half an inch. Leave one blank line before and after an extract.

If a letter runs over to a second page, follow the instructions in *Continuation-Page Heading* on page 151.

Complimentary close. A complimentary close is used in all formats except the simplified-block format. Place the close two lines below the message body, flush left in the full block format and at the page center or slightly right of it in the modified block format.

Capitalize the first word of the close, and place a comma after the last word. A close should be selected based on the relationship between the writer and the recipient. Although friendly, familiar closes are common in domestic business letters, more formality is required in international business letters.

Those who are on a first-name basis and have a close, personal relationship or a long working relationship commonly use informal closes, such as *Regards* and *Best regards*. When the persons have a friendly relationship but are not on a first-name basis, a close such as *Cordially* or *Cordially yours* is appropriate. The most neutral and most widely used closes are *Sincerely* and the somewhat more formal version *Sincerely yours*. When writing to a dignitary or high-ranking official and greater deference is needed, use a formal close such as *Respectfully* or *Respectfully yours*. (Whenever the word *yours* is added to a close, it tends to make it more formal.)

Signature. The signature block consists of the sender's printed name and, possibly, job title, as well as the handwritten signature. The information is positioned flush left in the full-block and simplified-block formats and at the page center or slightly right of it (aligned with the date at the top of the page) in the modified-block format.

When the signature block consists of the sender's name and, possibly, job title, place it about four lines below the complimentary close or five lines after the message body in the simplified-block format. If the sender's name is included with the letterhead data, however, it's not necessary to repeat it at the bottom of the page in the signature block.

When a company name is included (not common in the simplified format), place it two lines below the complimentary close, and place the person's name and job title about four lines below the company name. This form is used by accountants and others who want to make clear that the letter represents the company's, not the person's, opinion or report:

Sincerely yours,

WADE & SONS ACCOUNTING, INC.
Henry McCauley
Henry McCauley, CPA
General Manager

Write the handwritten signature the same as the printed signature. Thus if the printed signature is *Barry M. McCoy,* the letter shouldn't be signed *B. M. McCoy.*

Place a personal title, such as *Ms.,* in parentheses before the printed name only if the recipient otherwise would not know that the sender wants to be addressed that way (such as in international correspondence) or if gender isn't clear from the name alone. If you don't include a title, and if a recipient has no way of knowing if you hold a title such as *Dr.,* the recipient (in the United States) will assume that a man should be addressed as *Mr.* and a woman as *Ms.* However, recipients in other countries will address a woman as *Miss* or *Mrs.* if she doesn't put *Ms.* in front of her name in the signature block:

P. R. Thompson
(Mr.) P. R Thompson [*gender unclear*]

Rhoda Crossman
(Ms.) Rhoda Crossman [*letter to another country*]

If desired, include academic initials (*PhD*), initials designating a religious order (*SJ*), or evidence of certification (*CPA*) after the printed signature, even if a job title is also included. Place *Esq.* (*Esquire*), which is seldom used in the United States, after the name of a prominent professional man or woman if you know that the person prefers it:

Roger K. Sanders
Roger K. Sanders, PhD
Professor of Molecular Physics

Nadine M. Michaels
Nadine M. Michaels, Esq.
Attorney at Law

Even though the complimentary close is omitted in the simplified format, the signature lines—name and title—are included. Style them the same as for the full-block and modified-block formats, as indicated in the preceding examples.

Reference initials. The reference initials indicate who signs, dictates, and prepares the printout of a letter. Although this information is useful only to the sender, companies often put it on all copies, including the recipient's copy, to avoid having to add it later only on the file copies.

Place the initials two lines below the signature block. The computer operator's initials are written in lowercase letters. The composer/dictator and signer's initials are written in all capital letters. The reference initials and any notations that follow may all be single or double-spaced, depending on the length of the letter and personal preference. In either case, position the information flush left in all formats.

If the person who composes and signs a letter is the same, his or her initials are usually omitted. If the signer doesn't want to have his or her initials listed, you would note only the initials of the computer operator who prepares the printed letter. If different people compose, sign, and prepare the printout, all initials are usually given. Place the signer's initials first, then those of the person who composed or dictated the letter, and last those of the computer operator:

mj (*Composer/dictator and signer are the same, and this person doesn't want his or her initials listed.*)

AV:mj (*Composer/dictator and signer are the same, and this person does want his or her initials listed.*)

AV:MT:mj (*Composer/dictator and signer are different, and each person's initials are therefore listed.*)

Filename notation. Offices and file departments may find it helpful to have the filename added to a letter at the time of preparation to facilitate later storage and retrieval. If you include the name under which the letter will be filed, place the notation below the reference initials. If during an exchange of correspondence with an addressee you also include that person's filename, place it below yours. Add *Our file/ref.* and *Your file/ref.* for clarity:

mjacobs.ltr

Our file: mjacobs.ltr
Your file: bsimpson.doc

Enclosure notation. When you're enclosing other material, add a notation to that effect at the bottom of the letter, flush left, one or two lines below the filename or reference initials. (Space all notations consistently, either single- or double-spaced.)

Especially important enclosures should be identified. Spell out or abbreviate the words *Enclosure* (*Enc.*) and *Enclosures* (*Encs.*), as preferred. (Spell them out in international correspondence in case the recipient is unfamiliar with domestic US abbreviations.)

Enc.

2 Encs.: P & L Statement
       Policy ABC-123

Delivery notation. If you send a traditional letter by some means other than regular postal mail, add a notation below the enclosure notation specifying the form of delivery. If a letter is to be faxed and no cover sheet will be used (though a cover sheet is advisable), you may add a special fax notation centered two lines below the letterhead data or two lines above and aligned with the date. When the notation is in that position, write it in all capital letters or with an initial capital only, as preferred. Otherwise, write the notation with an initial capital only (except for proper nouns), and place it in the standard delivery-notation position below the enclosure notation:

> By certified mail
> By UPS Next-Day Air
> By fax to 800-555-4170

Copy notation. The copy notation is used to show who, other than the addressee, will receive a copy of the letter. Place the notation below the delivery notation, single- or double-spaced, the same as the other notations.

Common designations are *Copy* or *c* for any type of copy, *cc* for computer copy (formerly carbon copy), *pc* for photocopy, and *fc* for fax copy. When you send a copy to someone and don't want the addressee to know about it, use a blind-copy notation (*bc*). Omit the *bc* designation on the addressee's copy, and include it only on your file copy and the blind-copy recipient's copy.

> Copy: Marilyn Hartford
>
> cc: Harold T. Martin
>
> c: Lucille M. Baxter
>   Benjamin R. Taylor
>   Avery B. Wexler, Jr.
>
> bc: Jean McGhee

Postscript. A postscript, introduced by the initials *P.S.* (or *PS*), is a brief, additional comment unrelated to the principal message. It shouldn't be something you forgot to include in the main message. Place the postscript two lines below the last notation, flush left in the full-block and simplified-block formats and with a paragraph indent in the modified block format. Add the sender's initials at the end:

P.S. Have you heard when the next meeting of the Science Club is scheduled? DVC

Although more than one postscript should be avoided, if it's necessary to include two, use the abbreviation *P.P.S.* (or *PPS*) for the second one.

Continuation-page heading. If your message exceeds one page, use paper for the additional pages that matches the letterhead stationery. If your company doesn't have printed continuation pages, use matching blank sheets. Always carry at least two lines of the letter body over to the continued page. Reformat the first page if necessary to allow for this. Place a continuation-page heading a half inch to an inch from the top edge of the paper. Begin the continued text of the letter body two to four lines below the continuation-page heading. Format the heading in any basic style that you prefer, such as stacked or in a single line. Use the addressee's full name, without a personal title. Use figures or words for the page numbers, as preferred:

Mary Dennison, January 4, 20––, page 2

Mary Dennison
January 4, 20––
Page two

Memo and e-mail formats

A memo or e-mail format differs from a letter format in that it lacks an inside address, salutation, and complimentary close. Instead, guidewords, or headings, such as *Date, To, From,* and *Subject* are written at the top of the page, and the sender fills in the appropriate information after each word. Sometimes other headings, such as *Order Number* or *Attention,* are added to the basic guidewords.

Although traditional memos are often prepared on regular business stationery (8¹/₂ by 11 inches), commercial forms of various sizes are available in office-supply stores or can be ordered from printers. Commercial designs sometimes have ruled lines for the sender to handwrite a message rather than prepare it by computer. Certain styles have a carbonless attachment that the recipient can use for sending a reply on the same page as the sender's message. The following model for a traditional memo format would be appropriate for preparation on regular business letterhead. Although the e-mail format is similar (see the model on page 153), the e-mail software provides a standard template with certain guidewords after which information is filled in by the

---

COMPANY LETTERHEAD

DATE: February 4, 20—   **FROM:** Arthur J. Lee

TO: Janice B. Wilcox   **SUBJECT:** Traditional Memo Format

This is an example of a company memo with a displayed list. The other features and specifications are similar to those used for a traditional letter. The body also should be prepared the same as a traditional letter body.

Begin the message at least three lines below the last guideword (heading), and treat displayed lists something like this:

- Leave one blank line between the text and the first item in the list.

- Indent the list, or place it flush left, as desired.

- Leave one blank line between each item, if desired, but single-space within an item.

- Leave one blank line between the last line of the list and the first line of regular text.

You may—but don't need to—key in or handwrite your initials at the end of the message about two lines below the last line of text. Treat any concluding notations the same as those in a traditional letter.

AJL

jbwilcox.memo

cc: Mary Allen
    Sandra Kendall

Traditional Memo Format

From:	Arthur J. Lee ‹ajlassociates.com›
To:	Janice B. Wilcox ‹jbwilcox.com›
Date:	Thursday, February 4, 20—— 2:25 PM
Subject:	E-mail Format

Janice, this e-mail will serve as an example of a common e-mail format. It closely resembles a traditional memo format and also begins with guidewords, which are followed by the e-mail message.

As you can see, this message doesn't have any special formatting. Although lists, headings, and other features are widely used in traditional memos, it's uncertain whether any formatting you do in an e-mail will be translated the same way—or at all—by the recipient's software.

E-mails may have attachments (called "enclosures" in traditional mail) and may have some of the other parts used in a traditional memo, such as a copy distribution. Since there's no letterhead, you may want to add a signature block with address data at the end of your e-mail.

Let me know if you have any questions, Janice, and good luck with your report about e-mail communication.

****

Arthur J. Lee
Director of Communications
Arthur J. Lee Associates
114 Adams Drive, Room 4000
City, ST 98765
Phone: 420.555.4200
Fax: 420.555.4201
Website: www.ajlassociates.com

2/4/20——

E-mail Format

sender. The computer automatically fills in the date and time and the sender's name and e-mail address.

Fax cover sheets are sometimes styled like memos. Although companies usually design their own cover sheets, standard commercial forms are also available. Like memos, most include headings (*Name, Date, Address, Fax Number*, and so on) followed by a designated area where the sender can write a brief message.

Major parts of a memo or e-mail

The following are the main parts of a memo or e-mail: the confidential notation (traditional memo only); guidewords (*Date, To,* and so on); message body; the same notations used in a letter (reference initials, filename notation, enclosure notation, delivery notation, and copy notation); postscript; and continuation-page heading.

Like traditional business letters, traditional memos should be properly positioned on the page, using margins on all sides similar to those of a letter. The computer automatically provides standard (default) settings in an e-mail message. Your ability to change the default settings depends on the options of your e-mail program. Although memos may vary in size and arrangement of certain elements, a standard memo begins with the headings described below and ends with any notation or postscript.

Confidential notation. A confidential or personal notation may be used on a traditional memo if it contains sensitive material. Depending on the design of the memo, you might place the notation close to the top of the page, preferably above the guidewords. See the description of this notation on page 140 under *Major Parts of a Letter.*

Guidewords. The most common memo headings are *Date, To, From,* and *Subject.* But others may be added, as desired. In some e-mail programs, the template lists headings such as *To, Cc, Bcc,* and *Subject,* after which you fill in the desired information. Other information, such as *From* and *Date* (including time), are automatically provided by the computer. Again, other headings may be added, as desired. You may, for example, need one for an *Attention* line.

If traditional memo letterhead doesn't provide a fax number, an office telephone extension, an e-mail address, or a website, this information may be added beneath the last line of the letterhead data. One purpose of a traditional memo or e-mail is to provide essential information quickly and easily, so there is no restriction, other than appearance or practicality, on the number and variety of guidewords you include.

Guidewords may be printed on special memo stationery or

keyed in on your regular letter stationery. If you key in the headings, begin two to four lines below the letterhead data. Headings may be capitalized (*SUBJECT*), abbreviated (*SUBJ*), punctuated (*SUBJ.:*), or styled in some other way, according to preference. Each guideword, however, should be styled the same as the other guidewords.

To align the material that is filled in after each head on a traditional memo, begin writing one or two character spaces to the right of the longest head. In an e-mail message, the computer will align the information or set each item run on, depending on your program:

FROM: Ann C. Messenger<acmessenger@universal.com>
TO: Martin T. Phillips<mtphillips@northernlights.com>
DATE: January 4, 20--- 3:45 PM
SUBJECT: Executive Bulletin—March

If you're printing out and sending an original copy of a traditional memo to numerous people, type the word *Distribution** with an asterisk after the guideword *To*, or write "See Distribution" after *To*. Then, two lines after the last notation or postscript of the memo, repeat the word *Distribution*, and list each intended recipient by rank or in alphabetical order:

TO: Distribution*
TO: See Distribution

Distribution:
Martin Phillips, President
Jennifer Abbott, Director of Research
Steven Bartlett, Executive Assistant
Kenneth Hall, Research Assistant
Paula Kincaid, Research Liaison
Dennis Wolf, Administrator, Science Lab

Style the *From* name(s) on a traditional memo the same as you style the *To* name(s). Thus if you use initials only (*M. R. Danson*) with the *To* name(s), also use initials only with the *From* name(s). Although a memo has no signature, the sender may add his or her initials two lines below the body, flush left or slightly to the right, as preferred. Style (capitalize and punctuate) the other guideword information (*Subject, Attention,* and so on) as described previously for these elements in *Major Parts of a Letter,* beginning on page 139.

Body. The body of a traditional memo or e-mail should be handled the same as the body of a letter, as described in *Major Parts of a Letter.* However, a traditional memo and, especially, an e-mail are often more succinct than a letter, focusing on a single topic, for example (particularly in an e-mail message, which should be as brief as possible for easy reading on a computer screen).

Nevertheless, as in a letter, paragraphs in a traditional memo may be flush left or indented, and you may use subheads, lists, abstracts, and other display features. In fact, such features are often more common in a memo, which is intended to distill and provide factual information in a clear, easy-to-read format. For this reason, the memo format is used for short reports more often than the letter format. However, keep in mind that such formatting may be lost in an e-mail message if the recipient's software doesn't print it out as you've set it up.

Notations. In both a traditional memo and an e-mail, the reference initials (traditional memo), filename notation, enclosure notation, delivery notation (traditional memo), and copy notation should be styled as described in *Major Parts of a Letter.* An enclosure notation, however, is usually described as an *Attachment* in an e-mail. Whether you can attach text only or both text and graphics depends on your software. Follow the instructions of your program for selecting the material (file) that you want to attach to your e-mail.

Postscript. Place the postscript flush left or with a paragraph indent, the same as the style used in the body of a letter (in most traditional memos and e-mails, everything is set flush left). Begin two lines below the last notation, and follow the instructions given previously for styling a postscript in *Major Parts of a Letter.*

Continuation-page heading. For a traditional memo, use printed or blank stationery, and always carry at least two lines of the memo body over to the continued page. Follow the instructions given previously for styling a continuation-page heading in *Major Parts of a Letter*. In an e-mail, the computer automatically adjusts the copy and identifies continued pages as, for example, *Page 1 of 3*, *Page 2 of 3*, and *Page 3 of 3*.

Forms of address

The correct forms of address must be used in the inside address, salutation, and envelope address. The following sections describe the proper forms of personal, scholastic, official, and honorary titles.

Women. In domestic business correspondence, the most common title for single, married, widowed, and divorced women is *Ms.* (plural, *Mss.*). However, you may use the title *Mrs.* if you know that the woman prefers it. Don't address women in other countries by the title *Ms.* Instead, use the country's equivalent of *Miss* or *Mrs.* Most foreign titles, such as *Señora* or *Frau,* are spelled in full. The French *Madame,* however, should always be abbreviated before a personal name:

> Ms. Angela McCarthy and Ms. Laura Phelps
> Mss. Angela McCarthy, Laura Phelps, Dana Caruthers, and Nadene Pritkin
> Mme. Andrea Paix

The title *Madam* (plural *Mesdames*) is used primarily in formal correspondence to government officials and diplomats:

> Madam Ambassador
> Madam Prime Minister

If a woman holds another title, such as a religious, military, or scholastic title, use it in business correspondence rather than *Ms.*, unless you know that the woman prefers the personal title:

> The Reverend Angela McCarthy
> Captain Angela McCarthy
> Dr. Angela McCarthy

If you can't determine whether an addressee is a man or woman, omit the title:

A. R. McCarthy
[Address]

Dear A. R. McCarthy:

Men. The title *Mr.* (plural *Messrs.*) should be used unless a man has earned another title:

Mr. Leonard Eastman and Mr. Walter Grey
Senator Leonard Eastman and Mr. Walter Grey
Messrs. Leonard Eastman, Walter Grey, John Hudson, and
Wesley Stowe

Spouses. When addressing a business letter to spouses, use the same title for each spouse that you would use if you were writing a business letter to each person alone:

Mr. Leonard Eastman
Ms. Angela McCarthy-Eastman
Trinity Publishing
[Address]

Dear Mr. Eastman and Ms. McCarthy-Eastman:

Dr. Leonard Eastman
Dr. Angela McCarthy-Eastman
Trinity Publishing
[Address]

Dear Dr. Eastman and Dr. McCarthy-Eastman:

Dr. Angela McCarthy-Eastman
Mr. Leonard Eastman
Trinity Publishing
[Address]

Dear Dr. McCarthy-Eastman and Mr. Eastman:

Officials and dignitaries. *Esquire* (*Esq.*) is not common in the United States; however, it is occasionally used among attorneys and people in the consular corps. Omit the personal or other title when *Esq.* follows the name:

> Angela McCarthy, Esq.
> [Address]
>
> Dear Ms. McCarthy:

The Honorable is used before the names of certain prominent officials. Refer to the *Forms of Address Table,* beginning on page 160, for further examples:

> The Honorable Leonard Eastman
> [Address]
>
> Dear Governor Eastman:

Use of the title *Reverend* versus *The Reverend* depends on the person's religious affiliation. Some religious persons do not place *The* before *Reverend,* although most retain *The.* The examples in the Forms of Address Table use the traditional *The Reverend:*

> The Reverend Leonard Eastman
> First Unity Church
> [Address]
>
> Dear Dr. Eastman:

> Reverend Leonard Eastman
> First Unity Church
> [Address]
>
> Dear Dr. Eastman:

Use *Reverend* alone with a surname (no first name) only if a personal or scholastic title intervenes:

> The Reverend Ms. McCarthy
> The Reverend Dr. Eastman

Forms of Address Table

The following list gives the appropriate name and title to use in an inside address and the appropriate salutation for business correspondence. Use an official's business address for business and business-related social correspondence and the official's home address (when known) for social or personal letters and invitations. When a person holds a scholastic degree or honorary title, such as *Dr.*, substitute it for *Mr.* or *Ms.*

		Form of Address	Salutation
Academics	assistant professor	Professor Joseph/Jane Stone Mr./Ms./Dr. Joseph/Jane Stone	Dear Professor Stone: Dear Mr./Ms. Stone: Dear Dr. Stone:
	associate professor	Professor Joseph/Jane Stone Mr./Ms./Dr. Joseph/Jane Stone	Dear Professor Stone: Dear Mr./Ms. Stone: Dear Dr. Stone:
	chancellor, university	Dr./Mr./Ms. Joseph/Jane Stone	Dear Chancellor Stone:
	chaplain	The Reverend Joseph/Jane Stone	Dear Chaplain Stone: Dear Mr./Ms. Stone: Dear Father Stone:
	dean, college or university	Dean Joseph/Jane Stone *or* Dr./Mr./Ms. Joseph/Jane Stone Dean, School of ___	Dear Dean Stone: Dear Dr./Mr./Ms. Stone:

instructor	Mr./Ms./Dr. Joseph/Jane Stone	Dear Mr./Ms./Dr. Stone:
president	President Joseph/Jane Stone or Dr./Mr./Ms. Joseph/Jane Stone	Dear President Stone: or Dear Dr./Mr./Ms. Stone:
president/priest	The Reverend Joseph Stone President of _____	Sir: Dear Father Stone:
professor, college or university	Professor Joseph/Jane Stone or Dr./Mr./Ms. Joseph/Jane Stone	Dear Professor Stone: or Dear Dr./Mr./Ms. Stone:

Clerical and Religious Orders

abbot, Roman Catholic	The Right Reverend Joseph Stone Abbot of _____	Right Reverend Abbott: Dear Father Abbott:
apostolic delegate	His Excellency The Most Reverend Joseph Stone Archbishop of _____ The Apostolic Delegate	Your Excellency: My dear Archbishop:
archbishop, Armenian Church	His Eminence the Archbishop of _____	Your Eminence: Your Excellency:
archbishop, Greek Orthodox	The Most Reverend Joseph Archbishop of _____	Your Eminence:

	Form of Address	Salutation
archbishop, Roman Catholic	The Most Reverend Joseph Stone Archbishop of _____	Your Excellency:
archbishop, Russian Orthodox	The Most Reverend Joseph Archbishop of _____	Your Eminence:
archdeacon, Episcopal	The Venerable Joseph Stone Archdeacon of _____	Venerable Sir: Dear Archdeacon Stone:
archimandrite, Greek Orthodox	The Very Reverend Joseph Stone	Reverend Sir: Dear Father Joseph:
archimandrite, Russian Orthodox	The Right Reverend Joseph Stone	Reverend Sir: Dear Father Joseph:
archpriest, Greek Orthodox	The Reverend Joseph Stone	Dear Father Joseph:
archpriest, Russian Orthodox	The Very Reverend Joseph Stone	Dear Father Joseph:
bishop, Episcopal	The Right Reverend Joseph Stone Bishop of _____	Right Reverend Sir: Dear Bishop Stone:
bishop, Greek Orthodox	The Right Reverend Joseph Bishop of _____	Your Grace:

bishop, Methodist	The Reverend Joseph Stone Methodist Bishop	Dear Bishop Stone:
bishop, Roman Catholic	The Most Reverend Joseph Stone Bishop of ___	Your Excellency; Dear Bishop Stone:
bishop, Russian Orthodox	The Most Reverend Joseph Bishop of ___	Your Grace:
brotherhood, Roman Catholic, member of	Brother Joseph Stone	Dear Brother: Dear Brother Joseph:
brotherhood, Roman Catholic, superior of	Brother Joseph Superior	Dear Brother Joseph:
canon, Episcopal	The Reverend Canon Joseph Stone	Dear Canon Stone:
cantor	Cantor Joseph/Jane Stone	Dear Cantor Stone:
cardinal	His Eminence Joseph Cardinal Stone	Your Eminence:
clergyman/clergywoman, Protestant	The Reverend Joseph/Jane Stone *or* The Reverend Joseph/Jane Stone, DD	Dear Mr./Mrs. Stone: *or* Dear Dr. Stone:
elder, Presbyterian	Elder Joseph/Jane Stone	Dear Elder Stone:
dean of a cathedral, Episcopal	The Very Reverend Joseph Stone Dean of ___	Dear Dean Stone:

	Form of Address	Salutation
metropolitan, Russian Orthodox	His Beatitude Joseph Metropolitan of ____	Your Beatitude:
moderator, Presbyterian	The Moderator of ____ or The Reverend Joseph Stone or Dr. Joseph Stone	Reverend Sir: My Dear Sir: Dear Mr. Moderator: or My dear Dr. Stone:
monsignor, Roman Catholic (domestic prelate)	The Right Reverend Monsignor Joseph Stone	Right Reverend Monsignor: Dear Monsignor: Dear Monsignor Stone:
papal chamberlain	The Very Reverend Monsignor Joseph Stone	Very Reverend and Dear Monsignor Stone: Dear Monsignor Stone:
patriarch, Armenian Church	His Beatitude Patriarch of ____	Your Beatitude:
patriarch, Greek Orthodox	His All Holiness Patriarch Joseph	Your All Holiness:
patriarch, Russian Orthodox	His Holiness the Patriarch of ____	Your Holiness:
pope	His Holiness The Pope	Your Holiness: Most Holy Father:

president, Mormon Church	President Joseph Stone Church of Jesus Christ of Latter-Day Saints	Dear President Stone:
priest, Episcopal	The Reverend Joseph/Jane Stone The Rev. Dr. Joseph/Jane Stone	Dear Mr./Mrs. Stone: Dear Dr. Stone:
priest, Greek Orthodox	The Reverend Joseph Stone	Dear Father Joseph:
priest, Roman Catholic	The Reverend Joseph Stone	Dear Father: Dear Father Stone:
priest, Russian Orthodox	The Reverend Joseph Stone	Dear Father Joseph:
rabbi	Rabbi Joseph/Jane Stone or Joseph/Jane Stone, DD	Dear Rabbi Stone: or Dear Dr. Stone:
sisterhood, Roman Catholic, member of	Sister Mary Viventia	Dear Sister: Dear Sister Viventia: Dear Sister Mary:
sisterhood, Roman Catholic, superior of	The Reverend Mother Superior	Reverend Mother: Dear Reverend Mother:
supreme patriarch, Armenian Church	His Holiness the Supreme Patriarch and Catholicos of All Armenians	Your Holiness:

	Form of Address	Salutation
Diplomats		
ambassador, US	The Honorable Joseph/Jane Stone The Ambassador of the United States	Sir/Madam: Dear Mr./Madam Ambassador:
ambassador to the US	His/Her Excellency Joseph/Jane Stone The Ambassador of _____	Excellency: Dear Mr./Madame Ambassador:
chargé d'affaires, US	The Honorable Joseph/Jane Stone United States Chargé d'Affaires	Dear Mr./Ms. Stone:
chargé d'affaires to the US	Joseph/Jane Stone, Esq. Chargé d'Affaires of _____	Dear Sir/Madame:
consul, US	Joseph/Jane Stone, Esq. United States Consul	Dear Mr./Ms. Stone:
consul to the US	The Honorable Joseph/Jane Stone Consul of _____	Dear Mr./Mrs. Stone:
minister, US	The Honorable Joseph/Jane Stone The Minister of the United States	Sir/Madam: Dear Mr./Madam Minister:

minister to the US	The Honorable Joseph/Jane Stone The Minister of _____	Sir/Madame: Dear Mr./Madame Minister:
representative (foreign) to the United Nations (with rank of ambassador)	His/Her Excellency Joseph/Jane Stone Representative of _____ to the United Nations	Excellency: My dear Mr./Madame Stone: Dear Mr./Madame Ambassador:
representative (US) to the United Nations	The Honorable Joseph/Jane Stone United States Representative to the United Nations	Sir/Madam: Dear Mr./Ms. Stone:
secretary general, United Nations	His/Her Excellency Joseph/Jane Stone Secretary General of the United Nations	Dear Mr./Madam/Madame Secretary General:
undersecretary to the United Nations	The Honorable Joseph/Jane Stone Undersecretary of the United Nations	Sir/Madam: (if American) Sir/Madame: (if foreign) My dear Mr./Ms. Stone: Dear Mr./Ms. Stone:

	Form of Address	Salutation
Federal, State, & Local Government Officials		
alderman	The Honorable Joseph/Jane Stone	Dear Mr./Ms. Stone:
assemblyman/assemblywoman, state	The Honorable Joseph/Jane Stone	Dear Mr./Ms. Stone:
assistant to the president	Mr./Ms. Joseph/Jane Stone	Dear Mr./Ms. Stone:
associate justice, US Supreme Court	Mr./Madam Justice Stone	Dear Mr./Madam Justice: Sir/Madam:
attorney general, state	The Honorable Joseph/Jane Stone Attorney General, State of ___	Dear Mr./Madam Attorney General:
attorney general, US	The Honorable Joseph/Jane Stone Attorney General of the United States	Dear Mr./Madam Attorney General:
cabinet member	The Honorable Joseph/Jane Stone Secretary of ___	Sir/Madam: Dear Mr./Madam Secretary:
cabinet member, former	The Honorable Joseph/Jane Stone	Dear Mr./Ms. Stone:
chairman/ chairwoman, congressional committee	The Honorable Joseph/Jane Stone Chairman, Committee on ___	Dear Mr./Madam Chairman:

chief justice, US Supreme Court	The Chief Justice of the United States	Dear Mr. Chief Justice: Sir:
chief justice/associate justice, US Supreme Court, former	The Honorable Joseph/Jane Stone	Dear Mr./Ms. Stone: Dear Mr./Madam Justice Stone:
clerk, county	The Honorable Joseph/Jane Stone	Dear Mr./Ms. Stone:
clerk, of a court	Joseph/Jane Stone, Esq. Clerk of the Court of _____	Dear Mr./Ms. Stone:
commissioner (federal, state, local)	The Honorable Joseph/Jane Stone	Dear Mr./Ms. Stone:
director, federal agency	The Honorable Joseph/Jane Stone Director, _____ Agency	Dear Mr./Ms. Stone:
district attorney	The Honorable Joseph/Jane Stone District Attorney	Dear Mr./Ms. Stone:
governor	The Honorable Joseph/Jane Stone Governor of _____	Dear Governor Stone:

	Form of Address	Salutation
governor, former	The Honorable Joseph/Jane Stone	Dear Governor Stone: Dear Mr./Ms. Stone:
governor-elect	The Honorable Joseph/Jane Stone Governor-elect of _____	Dear Mr./Ms. Stone:
judge, federal	The Honorable Joseph/Jane Stone Judge of the United States District Court for the _____ District of _____	Sir:/Madam: Dear Judge Stone:
judge, state or local	The Honorable Joseph/Jane Stone Judge of the Court of _____	Dear Judge Stone:
librarian of congress	The Honorable Joseph/Jane Stone The Librarian of Congress	Sir:/Madam: Dear Mr./Ms./Dr. Stone:
lieutenant governor	The Honorable Joseph/Jane Stone Lieutenant Governor of _____	Dear Mr./Ms. Stone:
mayor	The Honorable Joseph/Jane Stone Mayor of _____	Dear Mayor Stone:

postmaster general	The Honorable Joseph/Jane Stone Postmaster General United States Postal Service	Dear Mr./ Madam Postmaster General:
president, US	The President The White House	Dear Mr. President:
president, US, former	The Honorable Joseph Stone	Dear Mr. Stone: Dear Mr. President: Dear President Stone:
president-elect, US	The Honorable Joseph Stone The President-elect of the United States	Dear Sir: Dear Mr. Stone:
representative, state	—*See assemblyman, state*	
representative, US	The Honorable Joseph/Jane Stone United States House of Representatives	Dear Mr./Ms. Stone:
secretary of state, for a state	The Honorable Joseph/Jane Stone Secretary of State, State Capitol	Dear Mr./ Madam Secretary:
senator, former (state or US)	The Honorable Joseph/Jane Stone	Dear Senator Stone: Dear Mr./Ms. Stone:

	Form of Address	Salutation
senator, state	The Honorable Joseph/Jane Stone The State Senate, State Capitol	Dear Senator Stone:
senator, US	The Honorable Joseph/Jane Stone United States Senate	Dear Senator Stone:
speaker, US House of Representatives	The Honorable Joseph/Jane Stone Speaker of the House of Representatives	Dear Mr./ Madam Speaker:
territorial delegate to the US House of Representatives	The Honorable Joseph/Jane Stone Delegate of _____, United States House of Representatives	Dear Mr./Ms. Stone:
undersecretary, of cabinet department (also deputy and assistant secretaries)	The Honorable Joseph/Jane Stone Undersecretary of the Department of _____	Dear Mr./Ms. Stone:
vice president, US	The Vice President of the United States or The Honorable Joseph Stone Vice President of the United States	Sir: My dear Mr. Vice President: Dear Mr. Vice President: or Dear Mr. Vice President:

Military Ranks*	Branch of Service	Form of Address	Salutation
admiral	USCG/USN	ADM Lee Stone, USCG/USN	Dear Admiral Stone:
brigadier general	USAF	Brig Gen Lee Stone, USAF	Dear General Stone:
	USA	BG Lee Stone, USA	Dear General Stone:
	USMC	BGen Lee Stone, USMC	Dear General Stone:
captain	USAF	Capt Lee Stone, USAF	Dear Captain Stone:
	USA	CPT Lee Stone, USA	Dear Captain Stone:
	USCG/USN/USMC	CAPT Lee Stone, USCG/USN/USMC	Dear Captain Stone:
chief warrant officer	USAF/USA	CWO Lee Stone, USAF/USA	Dear Mr./Ms. Stone:
colonel	USAF/USMC	Col Lee Stone, USAF/USMC	Dear Colonel Stone:
	USA	COL Lee Stone, USA	Dear Colonel Stone:
commander	USCG/USN	CDR Lee Stone, USCG/USN	Dear Commander Stone:
ensign	USCG/USN	ENS Lee Stone, USCG/USN	Dear Ensign Stone:
			Dear Mr./Ms. Stone:
first lieutenant	USAF/USMC	1st Lt Lee Stone, USAF/USMC	Dear Lt. Stone:
	USA	1LT Lee Stone, USA	Dear Lt. Stone:
general	USAF/USMC	Gen Lee Stone, USAF/USMC	Dear General Stone:
	USA	GEN Lee Stone, USA	Dear General Stone:

Military Ranks*	Branch of Service	Form of Address	Salutation
lieutenant	USCG/USN	LT Lee Stone, USCG/USN	Dear Lt. Stone: Dear Mr./Ms. Stone:
lieutenant (junior grade)	USCG/USN	LTJG Lee Stone, USCG/USMC	Dear Lt. Stone: Dear Mr./Ms. Stone:
lieutenant colonel	USAF USA USMC	Lt Col Lee Stone, USAF LTC Lee Stone, USA LtCol Lee Stone, USMC	Dear Colonel Stone: Dear Colonel Stone: Dear Colonel Stone:
lieutenant commander	USCG/USN	LCDR Lee Stone, USCG/USN	Dear Commander Stone:
lieutenant general	USAF USA USMC	Lt Gen Lee Stone, USAF LTG Lee Stone, USA LtGen Lee Stone, USMC	Dear General Stone: Dear General Stone: Dear General Stone:
major	USAF USA/USMC	Maj Lee Stone, USAF MAJ Lee Stone, USA/USMC	Dear Major Stone: Dear Major Stone:
major general	USAF USA USMC	Maj Gen Lee Stone, USAF MG Lee Stone, USA MajGen Lee Stone, USMC	Dear General Stone: Dear General Stone: Dear General Stone:

Rank	Abbreviation	Address	Salutation
rear admiral (lower half)	USCG/USN	RDML Lee Stone, USCG/USN	Dear Admiral Stone:
rear admiral (upper half)	USCG/USN	RADM Lee Stone, USCG/USN	Dear Admiral Stone:
second lieutenant	USAF USA USMC	2d Lt Lee Stone, USAF 2LT Lee Stone, USA 2NDLT Lee Stone, USMC	Dear Lt. Stone: Dear Lt. Stone: Dear Lt. Stone:
vice admiral	USCG/USN	VADM Lee Stone, USCG/USN	Dear Admiral Stone:
warrant officer	USAF/USA	WO Lee Stone, USAF/USA	Dear Mr./Ms. Stone:

*These military ranks and their abbreviations are used with the names of military officers. The abbreviated rank is followed by the full name, a comma, and the appropriate abbreviation of the person's branch of service (USAF for United States Air Forces, USA for United States Army, USCG for United States Coast Guard, USMC for United States Marine Corps, or USN for United States Navy). Example: ADM Lee Stone, USN. These forms of address apply to men and women; the first name *Lee* is meant to cover both sexes. Following are cadet/midshipman and enlisted ranks.

Cadets and Midshipmen

Rank	Address	Salutation
cadet	Cadet Lee Stone	Dear Cadet Stone: Dear Mr./Ms. Stone:
midshipman	Midshipman Lee Stone	Dear Midshipman Stone: Dear Mr./Ms. Stone:

Military Ranks*	Branch of Service	Form of Address	Salutation
Enlisted Personnel: A Representative Listing			
airman	USAF	Amn Lee Stone, USAF	Dear Airman Stone:
airman basic	USAF	AB Lee Stone, USAF	Dear Airman Stone:
airman first class	USAF	A1C Lee Stone, USAF	Dear Airman Stone:
chief master sergeant	USAF	CMSgt Lee Stone, USAF	Dear Sergeant Stone:
chief petty officer	USCG/USN	CPO Lee Stone, USCG/USN	Dear Mr./Ms. Stone:
corporal	USA	CPL Lee Stone, USA	Dear Corporal Stone:
	USMC	Cpl Lee Stone, USMC	Dear Corporal Stone:
first sergeant	USA	1SG Lee Stone, USA	Dear Sergeant Stone:
	USMC	1stSgt Lee Stone, USMC	Dear Sergeant Stone:
gunnery sergeant	USMC	GySgt Lee Stone, USMC	Dear Sergeant Stone:
lance corporal	USMC	LCpl Lee Stone, USMC	Dear Corporal Stone:
master gunnery sergeant	USMC	MGySgt Lee Stone, USMC	Dear Sergeant Stone:

master sergeant	USAF/USMC	MSgt Lee Stone, USAF/USMC	Dear Sergeant Stone:
	USA	MSG Lee Stone, USA	Dear Sergeant Stone:
petty officer	USCG/USN	PO Lee Stone, USCG/USN	Dear Mr./Ms. Stone:
private	USA	PVT Lee Stone, USA	Dear Private Stone:
	USMC	Pvt Lee Stone, USA	Dear Private Stone:
private first class	USA/USMC	PFC Lee Stone, USA/USMC	Dear Private Stone:
seaman	USCG/USN	SN Lee Stone, UCG/USN	Dear Seaman Stone:
seaman apprentice	USCG/USN	SA Lee Stone, USCG/USN	Dear Seaman Stone:
senior airman	USAF	SrA Lee Stone, USAF	Dear Airman Stone:
senior chief petty officer	USCG/USN	SCPO Lee Stone, USCG/USN	Dear Mr./Ms. Stone:
senior master sergeant	USAF	SMSgt Lee Stone, USAF	Dear Sergeant Stone:
sergeant	USA	SGT Lee Stone, USA	Dear Sergeant Stone:
	USMC	Sgt Lee Stone, USMC	Dear Sergeant Stone:
sergeant first class	USA	SFC Lee Stone, USA	Dear Sergeant Stone:

Military Ranks*	Branch of Service	Form of Address	Salutation
sergeant major	USA	SGM Lee Stone, USA	Dear Sergeant Major Stone:
	USMC	SgtMaj Lee Stone, USMC	Dear Sergeant Major Stone:
specialist, fourth class	USA	SP4 Lee Stone, USA	Dear Specialist Stone:
staff sergeant	USAF/USMC	SSgt Lee Stone, USAF/USMC	Dear Sergeant Stone:
	USA	SSG Lee Stone, USA	Dear Sergeant Stone:
technical sergeant	USAF	TSgt Lee Stone, USA	Dear Sergeant Stone:

Professions		Form of Address	Salutation
attorney		Mr./Ms. Joseph/Jane Stone Attorney-at-Law *or* Joseph/Jane Stone, Esq.	Dear Mr./Mrs. Stone:
dentist		Joseph/Jane Stone, DDS	Dear Dr. Stone:
physician		Joseph/Jane Stone, MD	Dear Dr. Stone:
veterinarian		Joseph/Jane Stone, DVM	Dear Dr. Stone:

There are as many reasons for writing as there are subjects to investigate—a paper or report may be undertaken as a school assignment, a job assignment, or a professional opportunity (presenting a paper at a meeting or publishing an article).

At times, a very specific topic is assigned to you. At other times, you may choose any subject that interests you. Often, you are asked to look into a general subject area and choose a specific topic within it. Whatever your reasons for writing, you want the final product to represent your best work.

It is the purpose of this section to provide general guidelines for research and writing that will help you from the preliminary stages to the final draft. Certain techniques will be useful to you in preparing papers on any subject and will be suitable for a wide variety of source materials.

Whatever the purpose of your writing, the final version will reflect how well you prepared yourself from the start. Trying to take shortcuts along the way will result in an inferior piece of work. Care and time invested during the preliminary stages will provide the foundation for a well-written essay or report.

Planning

There is a great deal of work to be done before you begin to write. A good way to begin is to formulate a tentative title (which may or may not be the final title of your paper). The tentative theme may be too broad or too narrow, or it may be a topic that you do not have the facilities to research. At this point, the title is merely a first statement of the general area of your paper and can help you focus your research.

By definition, all research papers are based on some kind of data; they also require that the writer collect, organize, present, and evaluate data. Some papers rely very heavily on other people's evaluations, while other papers rely more heavily on the writer's opinions. In either case, it is not enough simply to reproduce sources.

Before you commit yourself to a topic, consider the materials you will need: books, magazine articles, newspaper clippings, websites, maps, recordings, sheet music, statistics, informants, and the like. Begin to check libraries and the Internet to find out which resources are available to you and make preliminary inquiries about where to look for other sources. Can you find what you need in one library? If not, you will have to look farther afield, or you may have to restate your topic. On the other hand, it is possible—especially on the Internet—to find an overwhelming amount of information, in which case it is best to narrow your topic further.

Certain practical considerations should determine how you plan your research. For example, research that requires travel must be planned carefully. If you are generating your own experimental data, allow plenty of extra time in case something goes wrong. If you plan to interview experts for your paper, you'll need to schedule time with them well in advance. Sometimes it is necessary to wait for a reserved book or an interlibrary loan. Time must be allotted realistically. Some extra time should always be allowed for the unexpected.

Getting started

It is usually necessary to make some preliminary notes for an outline. These outline notes may be revised, expanded, or totally reorganized once your research is under way. The data you encounter may not be what you expect to find, or it may cause you to change your thinking and approach the subject from a different angle. Before you start to research your topic, you need to organize your ideas and make some preliminary notes.

Take one topic as an example:

> *What will the world's population be in the year 2025?*
> Reasons for asking the question
> Predictions:
> > On what basis are they made?
> > Do experts agree?
> > Are there areas of general agreement?
> > Are there areas of major disagreement?
> The unpredictable:
> > What events could alter predictions?
> > How likely are those events?
> > Have events ever altered past predictions?

Remember to keep notes of your own evaluations of the source materials you encounter.

As you begin to read, you may want to narrow the focus of your outline to stress a particular aspect of the topic:

> Shifts in the ratio of older people to younger people
> Relation of population growth to Earth's resources
> Differences in population trends in developed and developing nations

Begin your research by reading a general book or article about your topic. A quick Internet search can give you a good idea of the general scope of your topic and also lead to other areas to explore. Be sure to word your search carefully and reword if necessary. You may be fortunate enough to find an article or website that provides a good overall picture of the subject. Encyclopedias contain general articles written by experts in the field that will suggest different aspects you may want to investigate. Such general essays, whether in print or electronic, may provide a short list of sources you can use to get started on your own research. Each source you consult will lead you to others. As you proceed with your research, you will be sifting and weighing a lot of material. When you begin to do research, it's difficult to predict the direction in which the work will go. Often, it's not until you're well into the research process that you can decide how to organize the information you're finding. What seems significant at one point may not be worth including when you start to write.

One of the most difficult aspects of preparing and organizing information is deciding what to include and what to omit.

See *Guide to Research*, beginning on page 217, for finding materials on the Internet and in the library. A good resource for historical research is *The Modern Researcher*, Fifth Edition, by Jacques Barzun and Henry F. Graff.

Taking notes

As you work, you will need to keep notes of what you learn. Many people still find it easiest to take notes on index cards, while others take notes in a notebook or directly into a computer file.

If you are using the index card method, it is advisable to equip yourself with two kinds of index cards (either two sizes or two colors). One set of cards will be used to record your sources. Each card will represent a different source. The second set of cards will be used to take notes of specific information gained from a source. These cards will contain much of the substance of your paper. They will record quotes, opinions, analyses, and other data. They may also contain your own opinions of what you encounter.

With a notebook or computer file, it is advisable to keep notes on separate pages (whether paper or electronic) with a header showing the source for each note. There are also computer programs available that allow you to format your notes as virtual index cards.

In addition to the cards, some of your "notes" may be photocopies of library materials that you will need for reference. As you duplicate material for your reference, though, keep in mind the copyright laws that govern the extent to which you can legally photocopy copyrighted material. Photocopy machines usually have these laws displayed near them.

If you are working on a computer and have access to a full-page or hand-held scanner, you may be able to scan information from your sources directly into a file rather than relying on handwritten index cards. You can also copy and paste notes directly from Internet sources. In either case, remember to also copy as much bibliographic or identifying material as possible so that the information can be properly credited. When you copy a direct quote from a website, make sure to add quotation marks into your notes file to help you remember that the words were written by someone else and must be credited as such.

However you take your notes, exercise care and keep a comprehensive list of your sources so that you'll have the information you'll need for your bibliography or list of works cited.

Source cards. You should make out a separate index card for each source you consult or keep a complete list in a computer file. When the time comes to begin writing, you may not quote every book and article, or even refer to each specifically, but you may want to include additional sources in a footnote, endnote, or bibliography.

During the writing process, source cards provide the bibliographic data for your information cards; once the paper or report is finished, the same cards, alphabetically arranged, enable you to complete your bibliography or list of works cited. You can record your own general comments about each source on the appropriate card. And, because you have the full data on the source card, you will not need to repeat all the information on each information card.

In general, bibliographical information includes whatever your readers will need to know if they want to consult the same source. Usually this consists of the work's author, title, city of publication, publisher, and date of publication but may also include the translator, editor, edition, or volume. Always use the publisher's name as it appears and record only the first city listed. Periodicals, such as journals and magazines, will require both the article title and the title of the publication. Most of the bibliographical information for a book will be found on the title page and the reverse of the title page (the copyright page). Electronic sources, especially Internet sources, can be tricky to cite. Because websites move and Internet addresses can change, you must include not only the URL and date of access, but also enough other information to be able to find the material again through an Internet search engine. Maps, sketches, works of art, recordings, filmstrips, and any other materials you use also require complete bibliographical information. For information about presenting bibliographic information in your paper, see *Documenting Sources,* beginning on page 204.

Information cards. Most of your notes will record facts or opinions you encounter in your sources. Because some quotations may be quite long, consider using five- by eight-inch index cards if you are using paper. You may find yourself making a considerable number of information cards from one source and very few cards from another. Some notes will record specific statements, others will summarize ideas. Still others will contain brief quotations (in quotation marks). Because information cards contain different kinds of data, be sure to indicate whether the card contains a direct quotation, your paraphrase of the source, or your opinion of it. When you begin writing, these notations will tell you what information you need to put in a citation as well as what material you need to put within quotation marks (all whole or partial direct quotations). If you are copying text directly from a website or other electronic source, be sure to add quotation marks.

All cards or electronic notes should show the author's name and the page number(s) from which the data was taken. If you are using more than one book or article by the same author, the title may substitute for the author's name. Here you need only sufficient information to ensure that you give proper credit to your sources; you have full bibliographic information on your source cards or in your source file.

Much of what you learned in your research will not be taken in notes. You will be forming ideas about the topic and the manner in which you intend to pursue it. Before you reach the end of your research, you should be able to prepare an outline that will show the final plan of the paper you will write.

Making an outline

A substantial paper or report needs a well-balanced outline. In the finished product, the framework may be obvious or hidden, but it must be there. There are always several different methods for organizing information, so you may want to experiment before you settle on one way of outlining. For instance, if you're writing about someone's life or a nation's development, a chronological outline might seem to be the best way to organize your material, but you may try organizing the information to emphasize the person's achievements or the major industries of the nation.

A good outline has a structure of major divisions and subdivisions:

    I. Roman numerals (I, II, III, etc.) mark off the major divisions of ideas in the paper.

        A. Capital letters (A, B, C, etc.) are used to subdivide ideas within each Roman numeral group.

            1. Arabic numerals (1, 2, 3, etc.) subdivide the ideas within each capital letter group.

                a. Lowercase letters (a, b, c, etc.) form the subgroups within the Arabic numeral divisions.

It is not necessary to subdivide each topic. No topic, however, should have an *A.* subhead without also having a *B.* subhead.

Similarly, if there is a *1.*, there must be a *2.*; if there is an *a.*, there must be a *b.* In other words, if a category is to be subdivided, it should have at least two subdivisions.

The subdivisions within an outline should be balanced. The *I.* topic should be as important as the *II.* and *III.* topics. Within each further division, there should also be balance.

Let us examine some possible outlines for the subject "What will the world's population be in the year 2025?" Note that in each example below, the title and the basic point (major thesis) of the outline in the paragraph following the title have been restated to suit the particular subject eventually chosen. Your major thesis, or some version of it, should appear in your introductory paragraphs.

The following is an example of a phrasal outline. You may choose to use a phrasal outline to organize your paper. Here, the thesis is the only portion described in a full-sentence format.

PLANNING FOR AN OLDER POPULATION

All evidence indicates that the proportion of old people to young people in US society is increasing. The shift will require new planning for the future.

I. Evidence of the shift
    A. The declining birthrate
    B. The changing death rate
    C. Population profiles for the future
        1. Profiles based on current rates
        2. Profiles based on various predictions for the future
            a. Same birthrate, lower death rate
            b. Lower birthrate, same death rate
            c. Lower birth and death rates
II. Implications of the population shift
    A. For work and retirement patterns
        1. Current patterns
        2. Prospective patterns
    B. For government planning
        1. Government income
        2. Government services
        3. Need for public institutions
    C. For people planning careers
    D. For industries

III. Planning for the future
    A. Fitting current data into planning schemes
    B. Monitoring future changes
IV. Steps to begin to take now

Once you have settled on the structure of your paper, expand your phrases into sentences to make the writing process easier.

PLANNING FOR AN OLDER POPULATION

All evidence indicates that the proportion of old people to young people in US society is increasing. The shift will require new planning for the future.

I. Evidence of the shift in the ratio of older people in the population is available in our present statistics.
    A. The birthrate is declining because many women are choosing to have fewer children.
    B. The death rate is decreasing because more people are living longer.
    C. From present statistics we can provide a profile of future population ratios. All profiles will suggest an older population.
        1. We can project future population ratios by using the same birthrate and a lower death rate.
        2. We can assume a lower birthrate and the same death rate.
        3. We can assume both lower birthrates and death rates based on current trends.

II. The shift in the population, an increase in the number of older people, has important implications for future planning.
    A. We need to consider this shift in the population when we make projections about work and retirement patterns.
        1. Our projections must begin with an understanding of current work and retirement patterns.
        2. Based on current patterns, we can project how the increase in our older population will affect future work and retirement patterns.
    B. The government will need to consider the population shift in every sphere of its planning for the future.
        1. An older population will affect the amount of government income derived from taxation.
        2. An older population will mean a restructuring of

the government services provided, such as Medicare and Medicaid, and how money is allocated to such services.

    3. An older population will also mean an increased need for publicly supported hospitals, rehabilitation centers, and home-care providers.

  A. People planning careers will want to consider the requirements of an older population, such as increased leisure time and increased need for occupational therapy.

  B. People involved in industrial planning will also need to consider the different needs of an older population.

III. An increasingly older population will affect planning for the future.

  A. The trends indicated in current data will have to be incorporated into planning for the future.

  B. Planners will have to continue to monitor changes as they affect projections for the future.

IV. There are steps we can take now to incorporate this information into our plans for the future.

The expanded outline in sentence form is much clearer than the phrasal outline. A sentence outline can help to clarify thinking about a subject. It will reveal the strengths and weaknesses of the structure better than a phrasal outline will. If a sentence outline is well thought out, each topic may be incorporated into the essay or report as a heading, subheading, or topic sentence of a paragraph.

An outline will take various shapes depending on the nature of the data and the way you assemble it. By the time the outline is prepared, you should know what data is available. Sometimes the outline will reveal the need for additional information in particular areas.

Relating information cards to the outline. Each writer has a distinct style of relating information cards to the outline. Some people prepare the outline itself by arranging the cards to create a pattern. Other people develop a mental image of an outline as research progresses, then arrange the cards to suit the outline. Whatever system is used, at some point the cards must be organized to fit the outline. If your notes are in a computer file, it is often helpful—especially if your topic is complicated—to print them out, cut them apart, and rearrange the pages physically. It is advisable to make notations of pertinent subtopics on an upper corner or as an electronic header on each card.

A finished paper should never read like an assortment of cards. The data on the cards will be used indirectly in some instances and directly in others. Sometimes a card will merely serve as a way of reminding you to include an idea. Other cards may have been made before a final outline was drafted, and their data may be irrelevant to the final topic. Do not hesitate to eliminate irrelevant information. One of the most important aspects of planning a well-written, coherent report or essay is a sense of what is relevant and what is not. Irrelevant information detracts from the coherence of your writing and confuses your readers.

Writing

It is not necessary to be a great writer to produce a good paper or report. It is necessary, though, to have a good grasp of the major ideas, good information, and a good outline. By the time you are ready to write, you should be familiar with any words or terms currently used in the field and you should be capable of explaining them.

The most difficult part of a document to write is the first paragraph. A first paragraph may raise an interesting question that you will answer or attempt to answer later in the paper. It may propose an idea to be examined, argue a cause, state a conclusion, or do any of a number of other things. At times, a first paragraph may begin with a quotation that will serve as a theme for agreement or disagreement. Above all, the first paragraph should be interesting and should be related to the rest of the paper. Because your written work is likely to be revised several times before you consider it ready to be seen by others, you may find it easiest to write your introduction or opening paragraph after you've finished the report or paper.

Keep your writing as simple as possible. Use unfamiliar or technical words when they are appropriate, but do not try to introduce learned words just to sound learned. If the subject you are dealing with has its own vocabulary, use that vocabulary. Your goal is readability and understanding. Try to avoid sentences that must be read and reread to arrive at their meaning. During the process of revision, break such sentences into their components and rewrite them with greater clarity.

There should be a logical flow from sentence to sentence and paragraph to paragraph. One idea will flow into the next and your writing will be persuasive. Often when a flow of ideas is lacking, it is because the writer has not absorbed the material well and is simply recording one note after another. A logic should also exist from section to section of a work. Transition sentences or paragraphs prepare the way for the introduction of new subject matter.

Many people believe that clear writing is related to clear thinking. If you are having a great deal of trouble putting your thoughts into writing, reexamine your thinking. Are you confident of your ideas and your data? Can other conclusions be drawn from your work? If so, how will you deal with them? If you are not confident of your material, do you have enough time to do some more research? If not, can you redefine and limit your topic to material with which you are comfortable?

Good writers aren't born. Good writing is the result of discipline, attention to details, and lots of practice, and it is something that can be learned. An often overlooked requirement for excellent written work is revision, revision, and revision. The more you reread what you're writing, the more confident you will become; the more adept you become at spotting your own particular writing weaknesses and correcting them, the easier writing will become. One draft of a document, or even two drafts, is simply not enough. It is also helpful to have someone whose opinion you respect read over a later draft and point out places where your logic isn't clear or where there are weaknesses in your presentation.

The process of revision is considerably simpler now than it was in the past when changes were made by cutting up the typewritten pages and pasting or taping the revisions into their new location. Word-processing software allows you to cut, insert, and move text as you wish. Revising is now so easy that all writers should feel compelled to revise their material until it is as good as it can be.

Writing papers using a word processor typically involves these basic steps: format, input, edit, save, proofread (screen), print, proofread (paper), correct, save, print, and store. One of the most important but sometimes neglected skills is proofreading. Do not assume your spell-check program will catch all your mistakes. A spell-check program, for example, will accept the word *lose* as correct even if you really mean *loose*. It will also fail to warn you about *their/there, its/it's*, and about typographical errors that create other words, such as writing *then* for *than* or *ant* for *and*. These are problems you will have to watch for yourself. Before submitting any work, you should carefully read it over to check for any missed errors. If possible, have someone else read it over as well, since familiarity with the work makes it easier to miss errors and fresh eyes will probably catch some mistakes that you have missed. (See also *Proofreading,* beginning on page 213.)

Whatever the purpose of your writing, its preparation offers an opportunity for you to examine new topics, learn new research procedures, and sharpen writing skills. Some papers may be more successful than others, but over the years you will gain confidence and facility in preparing them.

Style and format

How you present your work affects the way your readers respond to it. A clean and inviting appearance is one of the most important considerations when putting a piece of writing into final form, whether you are composing an original paper based on your own research or organizing and styling a report based on another person's work. All job applicants know the importance of first impressions and hence the need to present a neat appearance when first meeting a prospective employer. Similarly, a cleanly printed and styled paper will encourage readers to take it seriously. A sloppy or careless presentation will, in contrast, indicate to your audience that you don't feel your own work is important. If you haven't bothered to make your work presentable, you cannot expect anyone else to want to read it.

What will the final piece look like? Much depends on the purpose and audience for the writing. Papers and reports can be written in either a formal or informal format. A formal paper, as you shall see, has a complex structure and often presents the results of original research or a compilation and synthesis of other people's work (secondary sources). Academic essays, business reports, and technical papers are all formal and require care and precision in their final presentation. An informal paper, on the other hand, may comprise only a short text with a title or a few pages of notes from which you improvise, depending on how well you know your topic. At its simplest a written presentation may take the form of a business letter.

Regardless of the format used, the following stylistic points should be observed:

- All papers and reports need a cover or title page giving the title, the name of the writer, the date, and the name of the class or organization to which the project is being submitted.
- All pages should be numbered in the same position, either centered at the top or in the upper-right-hand corner.
- All margins should be uniform, and they should not be skimpy.
- Any charts, graphs, or similar material should be numbered. A standard style for the title and legend of figures should be maintained.
- All sources you quote or borrow information from need to be appropriately documented using endnotes, footnotes, a bibliography, or a list of works cited. Consult a style manual for details on formatting. (See *Documenting Sources,* beginning on page 204.)
- Most papers and reports are typed or printed out on standard 8 1/2 by 11 inch white paper. Certain organizations or kinds of projects require the use of pre-ruled or otherwise nonstandard paper. In any case use only high-quality paper for your final copy, and be sure to use a high-quality printer.

The following sections describe the principal parts of a formal report, although not all formal reports include every part. Some, for example, may have no cover or flyleaves. Others may omit the letter of authorization or the acknowledgments page. However, a long, complex formal report should always have a title page and a table of contents in addition to the body and any material associated with the text, such as a list or table.

Front matter

Cover. If you use a cover, select one that will protect the paper for a long time and one that is appropriate for the overall length of the work. A ring binder, for example, is appropriate for a five-year plan consisting of hundreds of pages. The cover should contain a label bearing the title and the writer's name.

Flyleaf. Formal reports often have a flyleaf—a blank page appearing after the cover at the very beginning. Sometimes a paper may have two, one at the beginning and another at the end. Flyleaves protect the rest of the document and allow space for the reader to write comments.

Title page. This page contains the title of the paper, the name of the writer (and his or her position, if applicable), the name and address of the department or company (if the paper is written as a job assignment), the department and university or college (if the paper reports academic research), or the name of the class (if the paper is written as a school project), and the date. An informal paper usually dispenses with a full title page and instead has a cover giving the title, the writer's name, and sometimes the name of the company or class to which it is submitted. A formal paper may have both a title page and a cover.

Letter of transmittal. A letter of transmittal (or a cover letter) is more formal than, and is used in place of, a preface. It is printed on regular business letterhead. In addition to giving some or all of the information contained in an introduction, it is directed specifically to the authorization or request for the paper. Any acknowledgments, as of contributors, assistants, or sources that are not mentioned elsewhere, should appear in a separate paragraph at the end of the preface or letter of transmittal.

Table of contents. This lists the titles of the chapters or principal sections of the paper (and their numbers, if any are used); the subheadings or subtopics within each chapter or section; the appendix, bibliography, and index; and the page number on which each begins. Since the actual text of any paper always begins on page 1, all pages preceding the text (including the table of contents) are numbered in Roman numerals and should be so listed in the contents table if you choose to include them. Everything listed in the table of contents should be entered in the exact order in which it appears in the finished work.

The heading of the page, always centered, is *Contents* (*Table of* is now considered extraneous). The table itself begins an inch or two below the heading and is set up in outline form. Chapters, sections, and similar divisions are placed on the left side of the page and page numbers on the right. You may use a string of periods as a leader to connect the left-hand entry to the page number if you wish. In addition, many people use the subheadings *Chapter* and *Page* on top of the left- and right-hand columns, respectively.

List of tables and illustrations. Many papers make extensive use of tables and illustrations (all illustrations are individually referred to in the text as *figures*). These lists follow the table of contents and have the headings *Tables* or *Illustrations*. If the contents page is set with column subheadings, these lists should conform to style, using *Table* or *Figure* on the left and *Page* on the right. If the tables and figures are to be inserted later, you should indicate where they are to be placed in the text.

Foreword and preface. The foreword—written by someone other than the writer of the paper—comments on the work, usually with words of praise or a statement about the importance of the work. The preface—written by the author of the paper—is a short statement regarding the purpose, scope, and content of the study, often including a summary of the research and methodology that was used. These sections should be single- or double-spaced, the same as the body of the report. You should style and position the foreword and preface titles the same as all other main titles in the report.

Acknowledgments page. When other people or organizations have contributed to the report, a brief notation acknowledging their help, support, and work may be included. Acknowledgments of this type are included on a separate page, usually styled in one or two short, single-spaced paragraphs. The word *Acknowledgments* is stated in uppercase and lowercase letters or in all capital letters, the same as other chapter or division titles. Begin all titles the same distance from the top of the page. If the text paragraphs are single-spaced, double-space between them, and center and balance all of the material attractively on the page.

Abstract or summary. This is a brief synopsis, normally in one or two paragraphs, of the problem dealt with in the paper, the methodology used in examining it, and the conclusions reached. Once found almost exclusively in technical studies, the abstract is now widely used in academic and business papers. Its condensed form makes it useful in research and as accessible reference material; hence it has become one of the most important parts of a formal paper or report.

The text

The text, or body, of a paper or report should be logically organized and clearly written. An introduction states the purpose and scope of the project, the methodology used, pertinent background information, and a brief statement of the conclusions drawn. The discussion is a detailed study of the subject, presented as briefly and succinctly as possible. The final section of the text presents a full explanation of the conclusions and/or recommendations produced by the study.

Spacing. The body may be single- or double-spaced, but it's usually single-spaced when the paper is very long. Papers being submitted to a teacher or professor should almost always be double-spaced to allow for comments and corrections. As always, be sure to consult any guidelines you have been given.

Headings. Many writers choose to use different levels of headings in the body to present the information in a clear and orderly arrangement and assist readers in following it. A relatively brief or uncomplicated paper will usually require no headings. If well-planned, the framework should be apparent because the finished work is a logical and natural sequence of thought. A long or complicated paper, a technical report, or a promotional brochure, however, usually requires headings to distinguish among many topics and subtopics and to guide readers through your presentation.

If you are writing a paper or report from an outline, the outline itself will provide the headings and subheadings. If you are working from raw data or a rough outline, you will need to formulate headings. Headings should be brief and informative. Use a single word or a phrase instead of a complete sentence.

Three or four levels of headings are usually enough, but if a paper is very complex, one or two additional levels may be used. The author may use Arabic numerals (1, 2, 3, 4, and so on), Roman numerals (I, II, III, IV, and so on), or an alphabetical system (A, B, C, D, and so on) with the heading titles. Some papers, especially technical reports, are written using an outline system for headings. The following example has three levels of headings:

> 1.0 FIRST MAIN SECTION
>   1.1 First Main Subsection
>   1.2 Second Main Subsection
>   1.3 Third Main Subsection
>   1.3.1 First subunit
>   1.3.2 Second subunit
>   1.3.3 Third subunit
>   1.4 Fourth Main Subsection
> 2.0 SECOND MAIN SECTION

In this style of outline system, the decimals signal the heading level. Keep in mind that if you have a heading labeled *A, 1,* or *(a),* you must have at least one other heading in the same set, such as *B, 2,* or *(b).* A heading in one set should never stand alone.

Less technical papers commonly use formatting instead of labels to indicate the level of the header:

> **MAIN HEADING**
>   **Subheading**
>   Subsubheading
>   Subsubheading
>   **Subheading**
>   Subsubheading
>   *Most limited subcategory*
>   *Most limited subcategory*
>   Subsubheading
> **MAIN HEADING**

Remember that each category of heading should always be treated identically.

Quotations. You will most likely need to include quotations of various lengths in your final paper. Remember that each must be reproduced exactly as it appeared in the original source, including the original punctuation. If a quotation needs to be altered in any way, an addition should be clearly set apart in square brackets, and a deletion should be marked by an ellipsis (three spaced periods preceded and followed by spaces: " . . . "). If there is a misspelling or other error in the text to be quoted, that can be shown by adding *sic* (Latin for *thus*) in square brackets immediately after the error or, in parentheses instead of brackets, after the quotation.

Short quotations appear within quotation marks in the body of the text, but longer quotes need to be visually set apart. Any quotation of five lines or more should be single-spaced and indented, and quotation marks should not be used. Longer quotations are generally introduced with a colon at the end of the introductory phrase.

> In 2004, Federal Reserve Chairman Alan Greenspan, speaking before the Center for Strategic & International Studies in Washington, D.C., noted the dramatic rise in six-year forward futures prices for crude oil and natural gas:
>
>> These elevated long-term prices, if sustained, could alter the magnitude of and manner in which the United States consumes energy. Until recently, long-term expectations of oil and gas prices appeared benign. . . . The recent shift in expectations, however, has been substantial enough and persistent enough to influence business investment decisions, especially for facilities that require large quantities of natural gas.

When quoting multiple lines of poetry within a prose paragraph, use a slash (/) to separate the poetic lines.

> The poem "Infant Sorrow" by William Blake begins, "My mother groaned, my father wept— / Into the dangerous world I leapt" (1–2).

For more detailed explanations and examples of how to incorporate quotations into your work, you can consult any standard style handbook. For information on citations, see *Documenting Sources*, beginning on page 204.

Illustrations. Although your software program may provide automatic formatting for tables and certain types of figures, you may want to develop your own template (standard format). The following guidelines are widely accepted in formal documents.

Numbering. Number tables and figures consecutively from beginning to end (1, 2, 3, and so on) or consecutively within a chapter (1.1, 1.2, 2.1, 2.2, and so on). Place the number after the word the writer has chosen for the document, as in *Table 2, Figure 4.7, Exhibit 6,* and *Illustration 21.*

Text references. Refer to each illustration at the appropriate place in the text, such as "See Table 7 and Figure 14." Ideally, you will place the appropriate table or figure in the text at or near this place of reference. In some business documents, though, illustrations are collected at the ends of chapters or at the end of the document after the appendix. In all cases, the numbers and titles that are used should be consistent with the numbers and titles appearing on the list(s) of illustrations in the front matter.

Titles. Make table titles and figure captions as short as possible. However, you can add a descriptive line as a table subtitle, a figure legend, or a general note immediately after the body of the table or figure:

> Table 12
> Policy Claims by Age Group, 18–65
>
> Figure 9
> A Basic Accounting Cycle

Place a table subtitle on a separate line below the table title or on the same line, as preferred, usually separated from the title by a colon:

Table 2
Career Paths: Occupational Titles and Work Functions for
Various Office Positions

Also, place a figure legend (description or comment about the figure) on a separate line or on the same line, as preferred, separated from the caption (title of figure) by a period:

Fig. 3. Chronological Resumé. The chronological format starts with your latest job experience and works backward. Only inclusive years should be used, without months.

Footnotes. Format footnotes to a table or figure like text notes, described earlier, and place them immediately after the table or figure body. Like text footnotes, the notes to an illustration are often preceded by note numbers, letters, or sometimes symbols.

List a source note (introduced by *Source:*) stating the source (if any) of the information or illustration first, followed by any general note (introduced by *Note:*) that applies to the table or figure as a whole. However, don't place the word *Source* before a brief credit line for an illustration, such as *Courtesy J. R. Miller Co.*

List numbered or lettered notes after any general note, and place corresponding superscript numbers or letters at appropriate places in the body of the table or figure. However, don't place a note number or letter after a table or figure title. Instead, for comments about the title or the illustration as a whole, use a general note preceding the numbered or lettered notes.

Column headings. Make column headings in tables brief and descriptive. If necessary, include subheads, or use a two-tier "decked" head:

2001	
Country	No. of Delegates

Capitalize important words in column headings, and make them either singular or plural, as desired, except for the head above the stub (left-hand column), which should always be singular.

Body. Either single- or double-space the body of a table or figure. Usually, you should double-space the body of a very short table and single-space the body of a longer table. However, even when the body is double-spaced, single-space the notes beneath the body.

Back matter

Appendix. All supplementary materials, such as maps, charts, or graphs, that provide background to or amplification of the topic are listed in the appendix. If there are two or more appendixes, they should be distinguished by letters (capitals) or numbers (Arabic or Roman).

The appendix(es) are placed in the back matter immediately after the last text page of the report and before any notes, glossary, bibliography, or index. Style and format the opening page the same as the first page of a chapter or other division.

Notes. Notes are an important element in any paper or report because they can convey many kinds of information, including

- comments that are not part of the main idea
- recommendations for further reading
- additional evidence to substantiate an argument
- the source of quotations or borrowed information (For other methods of reporting bibliographic information see *Documenting Sources,* beginning on page 204.)

Although *footnotes* may be placed at the bottoms of the pages where they are referenced in the text, some writers prefer to collect them in a notes section placed after the appendix, where they are often referred to as *endnotes*. Sometimes, the notes that represent sources of quoted material are collected in a notes section, and those that represent additional comments (*expository* or *substantive footnotes*) are placed at the bottoms of the appropriate pages. (If you choose to use a different method of documenting your sources—such as recording sources parenthetically in the text—your notes will only contain comments.) Often, then, the source notes are numbered and the expository notes lettered. In either case, the numbering or lettering is usually consecutive within chapters (if any) or throughout the entire report, as preferred. The text letters or numbers that correspond to the footnote letters or numbers should be set as superscripts (raised elements) just after the pertinent text passage: "The market that year was static."[4]

Style and format the title of the notes section the same as the titles of other chapters or divisions in the report. Prepare each note in paragraph style, indented or flush left, the same as the text paragraphs, and place the letter or number preceding each note on the same line. Single- or double-space the notes the same as the body of the report. The following examples are taken from the journal *October*.

Text

This leaves [Guy] Debord with nothing but his name.[2] At practical as well as at symbolic levels, he has been literally excluded from the new family of his mother, and left without any inheritance.[3]

Notes

2. *Take your name and take care of yourself:* Debord's family novel could be reduced to such an injunction, and to some extent he has actually answered it, since he has worked his whole life to establish his reputation, his renown (*renom*). Of course, in his case it could only be a bad reputation, a bad name: to whom would he owe a good name?

3. On this issue, see my *Guy Debord: La Révolution au service de la poésie* (Paris: Fayard, 2001), pp. 23–31; translation forthcoming from University of Minnesota Press.

There are a number of ways to shorten the citations in your notes. Frequently cited sources can be abbreviated and listed parenthetically in the text. For instance, the *Collected Works of Edgar Allan Poe* might be abbreviated *CW*. Either mention the abbreviation in the note containing the first citation or include it in a list of abbreviations in the front or back matter.

14. "The Purloined Letter," in *Tales and Sketches, 1843–1849*, vol. 3 of *Collected Works of Edgar Allan Poe*, ed. Thomas Ollive Mabbott (Cambridge: Belknap Press, 1978), 827. Hereafter, refer-

ences to Poe's tales are from this volume or from vol. 2, *Tales and Sketches: 1831–1842,* and are cited as CW.

To avoid repeating information in consecutive notes, you can use the abbreviation *Ibid.* (from Latin *ibidem,* "in the same place") to refer to the immediately preceding note.

> 18. Georg Lukács, *History and Class Consciousness: Studies in Marxist Dialectics,* trans. Rodney Livingstone (Cambridge, MA: MIT Press, 1971), 166.
> 19. Ibid., 74–82.
> 20. Ibid.
> 21. Ibid., 98.

A short reference (author's last name and shortened title) can be used to refer to a previous note other than the one immediately preceding. In the example below, note 8 refers back to note 6.

> 6. David "Honeyboy" Edwards, *The World Don't Owe Me Nothing: The Life and Times of Delta Bluesman Honeyboy Edwards* (Chicago: Chicago Review Press, 1997), 4–5.
> 7. Richard Wright, *Black Boy (American Hunger)* (1945; reprint, New York: HarperPerennial, 1993), 161.
> 8. Edwards, *The World Don't Owe Me Nothing,* 24.

Short references can also be used to refer to entries in the bibliography. For examples, see pages 207–208 of the *Documenting Sources* section.

Glossary. A glossary is placed before the bibliography or list of references. It's an alphabetical list of special terms used in the document, sometimes including additional terms pertinent to the subject, along with the definitions.

A glossary should be formatted the same as other main divisions, with consistent spacing and margins. The style adopted for the entries may vary, although terms are usually set in an italic or a boldface type:

> **diode** A device that permits electric current to pass in one direction but not the other.

Bibliography or list of works cited. A bibliography is an alphabetical list of books and other material consulted by the writer of the work in which the bibliography appears. If it includes only works referred to in the text or appearing in the notes, it may be called *Works Cited* or *References*. If it includes other works, it is usually called *Bibliography* or *Selected Bibliography*.

The list is placed at the end of the book, report, or other document after the glossary or, if there is no glossary, after the notes section. A hanging-indent format (flush and hang) is usually used, with the first line flush left and runover lines indented about half an inch to an inch, the same as a paragraph indent. Entries are listed alphabetically by author (if the work has an author) and a long dash (three em dashes) is used for repeated authors' names in succeeding entries. Here is an excerpt from a bibliography. (See *Documenting Sources*, page 204, for more information.)

Maddox, Jerald C. *Walker Evans: Photographs for the Farm Security Administration, 1935–1938*. New York: Da Capo, 1973.

Mora, Gilles, and John T. Hill. *Walker Evans: The Hungry Eye*. New York: Harry N. Abrams, 1993.

————. *Walker Evans: Havana, 1933*. New York: Pantheon, 1989.

Papageorge, Tod. *Walker Evans and Robert Frank: An Essay on Influence*. New Haven: Yale University Art Gallery, 1981.

Index. An index is an alphabetical list of all the significant topics and individuals discussed in a paper, report, book, article, or other document, with the numbers of all the pages on which a specific subject or person is mentioned. It is made from the page proofs or final copy of a printed work to ensure that all page numbers are final, and it enables readers to consult specific topics in your work. In general, indexes are prepared only for long works of nonfiction, not for papers, articles, or reports under 100 pages.

You can develop an index manually or by computer, or you may hire an outside professional indexer. With the appropriate indexing and sorting software, your computer will alphabetize and format the entries and check cross-references. If you don't use an indexing service, don't have indexing software, and want to prepare an index manually, you'll need a three- by-five inch index card file with alphabetical dividers.

Selecting the entries. Take a final copy of the document (a set of page proofs), and on each page underline words and phrases that will become main entries or subentries. Select nouns, such as *budget*, rather than adjectives or other parts of speech, such as *excessive*.

Most indexes have a combination of main entries and one level of subentries:

> input systems
>> for computers, 22, 53–63
>> optical character recognition for, 16
> input-output units, 53–63

In the preceding example, *input systems* and *input-output units* are main entries. The first word of an entry is often written with a small (lowercase) letter, unless it's a proper noun. Main entries are arranged alphabetically by the first keyword.

Like main entries, subentries, which represent topics of secondary importance, are composed of headings and page numbers. Place the subentries under the main entries with which they're associated. Arrange them alphabetically by the first keyword, and indent them an additional amount. Also, lowercase all subentries, unless they contain proper nouns. In the previous example, *for computers* and *optical character recognition* for are subentries.

Some indexers devise a system to distinguish entries and subentries while underlining keywords on page proofs during the initial step. They may, for example, check any underlined item that they believe will be a main entry. Whether you prefer to make such decisions while underlining keywords or later, it's important initially to write only one item on a three- by five-inch card.

Combining items. After you've underlined all appropriate items on the page proofs, transfer each underlined word to a separate index card, and after the word, write the page number where it appears. Eventually, you may have several cards for a single item or word, each with a different page number. After all underlined items have been recorded on cards, combine on a single card the page numbers from all cards that list the same item or word.

Arrange the cards by subject before you alphabetize them. For example, collect all cards pertaining to "input systems" together. If the decision about which item is a main entry was not made during the underlining step, make that decision now, and group the items that will become subentries *behind* the card for the main entry. Then arrange all main entry cards in alphabetical order, and arrange all subentry cards in alphabetical order behind each main entry.

Editing. Once you have the cards organized alphabetically, you can begin editing and polishing. For example, the subentry card behind the main entry *input systems* may say only *computers*, and you may decide to add the word *for* in front of *computers*:

> Input systems
>   for computers, 22, 53–63

If you haven't already combined the various cards with pages numbered 22 and 53 through 63, do so now. Next, add any cross-references that are needed:

> Input, 35, 61. See also input systems.

Edit all main entries and subentries for consistency in capitalization and punctuation. When you're satisfied that the index is complete and accurate, enter it in the computer, using the same general spacing, margins, and so on used for the rest of the report.

Documenting sources

A paper or report that makes use of material from outside sources requires notes, a bibliography, or a list of works cited with full bibliographic details for those works. Such details generally include author, title, city of publication, publisher, and date, and sometimes translator, editor, edition, or volume. A bibliography listing every work you consulted is optional; however, you at least need to provide the bibliographic details for the sources of the information you borrowed. This will require you to use notes (footnotes or endnotes) or a list of works cited. The following kinds of information must have attributions:

- quotations, charts, tables, graphs, or statistics that you copy as found
- borrowed ideas, arguments, facts, or other data that you present in your own words or in diagrams
- anything that is not gleaned from your own original research or analysis and is not common knowledge.

Before you begin, you should select a style for documenting your sources. Most style manuals specify

- how passages are attributed in the text
- where the full bibliographic information is located in the paper
- what information is included, and
- how that information is presented.

They contain detailed instructions for citing almost every conceivable kind of source, from a journal article with multiple authors to musical scores and online magazines. Be sure to consult with your professor or the organization to which you are submitting the paper about whether a style is preferred. Whichever style you choose, it is important to be consistent.

The most popular style manuals are published by the University of Chicago Press, the Modern Language Association (MLA), the American Psychological Association (APA), and the American Medical Association (AMA). Their titles are listed below with full bibliographic information, as if they appeared in a list of works cited. Each entry is formatted according to the manual represented. While all of these styles recommend including the same basic information, they differ on punctuation, placement, and typeface.

University of Chicago Press. *The Chicago Manual of Style*, 15th ed. Chicago: University of Chicago Press, 2003.

Gibaldi, Joseph. <u>MLA Style Manual and Guide to Scholarly Publishing</u>. 2nd ed. New York: Modern Language Association of America, 1998.

American Psychological Association. (2001). *Publication manual of the American Psychological Association* (5th ed.). Washington, DC: American Psychological Association.

1. Iverson C, Flanagan A, Fontanarosa PB, et al. *American Medical Association Manual of Style*. 9th ed. Philadelphia, Pa: Lippincott Williams & Wilkins; 1998.

Aside from the specifics of formatting bibliographic information, there are basically two methods for attributing borrowed material. One is to provide essential bibliographic information (author, date, and page number) parenthetically in the text following the borrowed material, and to list the more complete bibliographic information for each source at the end of the document in a separate section labeled *Works Cited* or *References*. This is commonly known as the *parenthetical citation* system or the *author-date* system. The other method is to put the bibliographic information in footnotes or endnotes, giving numerical references to these notes in the text. The note system only requires a separate list of sources (i.e., a list of works cited or a bibliography) if the bibliographic information in the notes is not complete.

While the Chicago style treats both systems equally, MLA and APA advocate the use of parenthetical citations, and AMA recommends a hybrid system. Traditionally, parenthetical citations have been used by writers in the physical, natural, and social sciences, and notes by those in history, literature, and the arts—though there are many exceptions.

The following samples illustrate the four major styles as they apply to the bibliographic information in the text and in the back matter. For general information on formatting notes, a bibliography, and a list of works cited, see the relevant sections in *Back Matter*.

Chicago style. Below are some examples of the Chicago style. The first example, taken from the journal *boundary 2*, consists of a text passage with references to notes.

Text

"Their enthusiasm for the new procedures waned as the protection of civil and political . . . rights . . . emerged as the priority consideration and many of them became the targets . . . for the Commission's new mandate."[3] For the eighteenth-century Declaration of the Rights of Man and of Citizens by the National Assembly of France, the "nation is essentially the source of sovereignty; nor can any individual, or any body of men, be entitled to any authority which is not expressly derived from it."[4] A hundred and fifty years later, . . . the human rights aspect of postcoloniality has turned out to be the breaking of the new nations, in the name of their breaking-in into the international community of nations.[5] This is the narrative of international maneuvering. Thomas Risse, Steven Ropp, and Kathryn Sikkink's recent book, *The Power of Human Rights*, takes the narrative further. In addition to the dominant states, they argue, . . . it is the transnational agencies, plus nongovernmental organizations (NGOs), that subdue the state.[6]

Notes

3. Mel James, "Country Mechanisms of the United Nations Commission on Human Rights," in *The Universal Declaration of Human Rights: Fifty Years and Beyond*, ed. Yael Danieli, Elsa Stamatopoulou, and Clarence J. Dias (Amityville, NY: Baywood Publishing, Inc., 1999), 76–77.

4. Cited in Thomas Paine, *Rights of Man* (Indianapolis, Ind.: Hackett, 1992), 79.

5. The identity of the nation and the state is generally associated with the Peace of Westphalia (1648), often thought of as one of the inaugurations of the Enlightenment. See, for example, R. Paul Churchill, "Hobbes and the Assumption of Power," in *The Causes of Quarrel: Essays on Peace, War, and Thomas Hobbes*, ed. Peter Caws (Boston: Beacon Press, 1988), 17.

6. Thomas Risse, Stephen C. Ropp, and Kathryn Sikkink, eds., *The Power of Human Rights: International Norms and Domestic Change* (New York: Cambridge University Press, 1999).

To conserve space in footnotes, Chicago recommends using *short citations*. Here short citations refer to entries in the bibliography.

Notes

4. Habermas, *Between Facts and Norms*, 47.

5. Ibid., 32.

6. Benjamin, *The Arcades Project*, 267–70.

7. Habermas, *Truth and Justification*, 52.

Bibliography

Benjamin, Walter. *The Arcades Project.* Translated by Howard Eiland. Cambridge, MA: MIT Press, 2000.

Habermas, Jürgen. *Between Facts and Norms: Contributions to the Discourse Theory of Law and Democracy.* Cambridge, MA: MIT Press, 1996.

———. *Truth and Justification.* Translated by Barbara Fultner. Cambridge, MA: MIT Press, 2003.

Chicago also provides guidelines for *parenthetical citations.* In this system, the author and the date of publication are provided in parentheses within the text. For instance, the short references in the example above would appear as follows:

(Habermas 1996, 47)
(Habermas 1996, 32)
(Benjamin 2000, 267–70)
(Habermas 2003, 52)

Instead of referring to a bibliography, parenthetical citations refer to a section titled *References.* Notice that in this section the date immediately follows the name of the author(s).

References

Benjamin, Walter. 2000. *The Arcades Project.* Translated by Howard Eiland. Cambridge, MA: MIT Press.

Habermas, Jürgen. 1996. *Between Facts and Norms: Contributions to the Discourse Theory of Law and Democracy.* Cambridge, MA: MIT Press.

———. 2003. *Truth and Justification.* Translated by Barbara Fultner. Cambridge, MA: MIT Press.

MLA style. MLA prefers the parenthetical citation system over the note system. Unlike other styles that use this system, however,

MLA does not include the date of publication in the parenthetical citation. Only the name of the author and the page number (if they are not mentioned in the text) are listed in the parentheses. To distinguish between more than one work by the same author, a shortened version of the title is given.

Text

When the fictional private detective Sherlock Holmes first appeared in <u>Strand</u> magazine in 1885 he was well received by the public as a figure "at odds" with this new police establishment. "From amateur detectives like Dupin and Holmes to the spate of professional private investigators and agency operatives who are their twentieth-century successors, it has become a convention of the genre to portray the sleuth at odds with the established police force" (Black 42). . . . Like Edgar Allan Poe's detective figure 'Dupin,' his process of detection is taken directly from Aldous Huxley's method of deduction: "observation of facts, including artificial observation, or experiment; comparison and classification of facts into general propositions; deduction; verification" (Smith 228). . . . As Rosemary Jann suggests in her essay "Sherlock Holmes Codes the Social Body," "Holmes' 'imagination' is guided by the thorough predictability of human behavior" (689). . . . Within this sphere, there is no space for the individual: "Only in reading against the grain of his deductions will we be able to escape Dupin's mind and enter the world detection flees" (Van Leer 88).

Works Cited

Black, Joel. <u>The Aesthetics of Murder.</u> Baltimore: Johns Hopkins UP, 1991.

Jann, Rosemary. "Sherlock Holmes Codes the Social Body." <u>ELH</u> 57. (1990): 685–708.

Smith, Jonathan. <u>Fact and Feeling: Baconian Science and the Nineteenth-Century Literary Imagination.</u> Madison: U of Wisconsin P, 1994.

Van Leer, David. "Detecting Truth: The World of the Dupin Tales." <u>New Essays on Poe's Major Tales.</u> Ed. Kenneth Silverman. Cambridge: Cambridge UP, 1993.

APA style. APA uses parenthetical citations containing the author's last name and the date of publication (page numbers are sometimes given as well). The following example is from the *Journal of Consulting and Clinical Psychology*, an APA publication.

Text

Universal interventions for preventing depression typically have been conducted in schools and have included as many as 1,500 children (Spence, Sheffield, & Donovan, 2003). The format usually has involved large-group presentations or curricular modifications. General strengths associated with universal interventions include avoiding the stigma of singling out individuals for treatment and relatively low dropout rates (Spence et al., 2003). Universal prevention programs with adolescents (e.g., Clarke, Hawkins, Murphy, & Sheeber, 1993) have focused on cognitive and behavioral skills training, including cognitive restructuring, anxiety management, relaxation, problem-solving skills, emotion-focused coping, anticipating consequences, and assertiveness. Universal interventions with elementary school-age children (e.g., Ialongo et al., 1999; Kellam et al., 1994) have sought to prevent depression by implementing mastery learning and behavioral management programs.

References

Clarke, G. N., Hawkins, W., Murphy, M., & Sheeber, L. B. (1993). School-based primary prevention of depressive symptomatology in adolescents: Findings from two studies. *Journal of Adolescent Research, 8,* 183–204.

Ialongo, N. S., Werthamer, L., Kellam, S. G., Brown, C. H., Wang, S., & Lin, Y. (1999). Proximal impact of two first-grade preventive interventions on the early risk behaviors for later substance abuse, depression, and antisocial behavior. *American Journal of Community Psychology, 27,* 599–641.

Kellam, S. G., Rebok, G. W., Mayer, L. S., Ialongo, N., & Kalodner, C. R. (1994). Depressive symptoms over first grade and their response to a developmental epidemiologically based preventive trial aimed at improving achievement. *Development and Psychopathology, 6,* 463–481.

Spence, S. H., Sheffield, J. K., & Donovan, C. L. (2003). Preventing adolescent depression: An evaluation of the Problem Solving for Life program. *Journal of Consulting and Clinical Psychology, 71,* 3–13.

AMA style. AMA combines aspects of a note system and a parenthetical citation system. Each entry in the reference list is numbered. Unlike most note styles, AMA permits multiple text references to the same entry, resulting in nonsequential numbering. The following example is from the *Journal of the American Medical Association*. (Reference number 13 has previously been cited.)

Text

The investigation of inflammatory biomarkers in AMD is rendered even more biologically plausible by the observation that inflammation is associated with angiogenesis and that neovascularization can occur in inflammatory eye diseases,[14] similar to the most advanced and debilitating neovascular form of AMD. Furthermore, in addition to CVD, stroke and Alzheimer disease may also have an inflammatory component.[13, 15] It is possible that AMD represents another chronic, age-related inflammatory disease that is manifested in the eye and other organs, including the heart and brain. Therefore, we examined the relationship between CRP levels and AMD in the multicenter Age-Related Eye Disease Study (AREDS).

References

13. Ridker PM. Clinical application of C-reactive protein for cardiovascular disease detection and prevention. *Circulation*. 2003;107:363–369.

14. Hawkins B, Alexander J, Schachat A. *Ocular Histoplasmosis: Retina*. 3rd ed. Vol 2. St Louis, Mo: Mosby Inc; 2001:1687–1701.

15. Akiyama H, Barger S, Barnum S, et al. Inflammation and Alzheimer's disease. *Neurobiol Aging*. 2000;21:383–421.

Plagiarism

Plagiarism is the intentional or inadvertent use of someone else's words or ideas without attribution. Theft of intellectual property (words and ideas) is illegal as well as unethical, and the consequences can include expulsion from school or the loss of a job. As you consult your sources it is imperative that you be aware at all times of which words and ideas are your own and which need to be attributed to someone else. In this age of easily accessible and copyable information, it can seem as though proper attribution is not necessary and plagiarism is not traceable, but this is not the case. In fact, while the Internet has made it easier to inadvertently plagiarize, Internet search engines have also made it easier to catch plagiarists. Extreme care must be taken throughout the writing process to ensure that your paper is ethically as well as academically rigorous.

At one time or another everyone has done some simple proof-reading, such as reading over a letter to see that everything is correct or checking over a list to see that nothing has been omitted.

The act of proofreading involves checking a typed or printed piece of copy against the original manuscript. Strict proofreading involves marking corrections in copy with textual symbols and marginal notations. Knowing how to use proofreaders' marks is helpful if you are proofing academic or office materials before or after they are typed or printed by someone else. While there is no single preferred method used in proofreading, there are basic guidelines.

Take as much time as you need to ensure accuracy. Most copy to be proofread, especially material that comes from a compositor, has very few mistakes. It is as easy to miss errors in clean copy as it is in dirty copy.

Read the copy through to the end once to understand its meaning, then forget about meaning. While some people appreciate suggestions, for example, of how wording could be improved, the proofreader's primary responsibility is to see that everything that is supposed to be in the text is in it and that the material is correct in all respects, such as spelling and spacing.

It is a good idea to read through the copy a number of times, checking for different things on each pass (such as spelling and punctuation or spacing and alignment). Read the copy three or four characters at a time, saying each letter, punctuation mark, and word space aloud. Remember that a misplaced comma is as crucial an error as a misspelled word. Complicated material, such as intricate tables and charts, is best proofread by two people, one reading from the original while the other checks the copy.

Take nothing for granted. Spelling and punctuation errors are missed by the proofreader who does not check every single word or mark about which he or she is unsure. Remember that even the original copy can contain spelling errors. Important pieces of copy should receive a second proofreading by another proofreader.

A sample of marked copy follows along with a chart of proofreaders' marks.

Sample copy

It is the proofreaders job to ensure that all typed or printed ma terial is properly spaced and aligned and contains grammatical typographical, or spellng errors. Mark all corrections in a color that is clearly distinguished that from of the copy Each correction requires a symbol in the text and a corresponding explanation in the marginnext to the line in which it is ffound. if there are 2 or more corrections in one line, write them in the margin the proper order and separate then with a slanting line Material to be inserted is written in the margin and its place is indicated by a caret. If you make you make an improper correction — and these things do happen do not erase it put a series of periods below what you have mistakenly crossed out in the text and write stet which means "Let it stand" in the margin.

¶ Always remember to take your time. The proofreader has one goal total accuracy. Never assume or guess that something is Right. Check every word whose spelling you are unsure of in your copy of The American Heritage® Dictionary of the English Language, Fourth Edition.

Proofreaders' marks

Instruction	Mark in Margin	Mark in Type
Delete	ℓ	the ~~written~~ word
Insert indicated material	good	the ∧word
Let it stand	stet	the ~~written~~ word
Make capital	cap	the word
Make lowercase	lc	ⱦhe Word
Set in small capitals	SC	See word
Set in italic type	ital	The word is word.
Set in roman type	rom	the word
Set in boldface type	bf	the entry word
Set in lightface type	lf	the entry word
Transpose	tr	the word right
Close up space	⌒	the wo rd
Delete and close up space	⌐	the wöord
Spell out	sp	2 words
Insert space	#	the word
Insert period	⊙	This is the word ∧
Insert comma	∧	words ∧words, words
Insert hyphen	‿=⁀/‿=⁀	word for word test ∧ ∧
Insert colon	⊙	The following words ∧
Insert semicolon	;	Scan the words ∧skim the words.
Insert apostrophe	∨	Johns words
Insert quotation marks	℣/℣/	the word ᵛword ᵛ
Insert question mark	?	the word ∧
Insert parentheses	(/)	The word word is in parentheses ∧. ∧
Insert brackets	[/]	He read from the Word the Bible. ∧ ∧
Insert en dash	⊥/N	1964 1972
Insert em dash	⊥/M ⊥/M	A dictionary how often it is needed belongs in every home. ∧

Instruction	Mark in Margin	Mark in Type
Start paragraph	¶	"Where is it?" "It's on the shelf."
Move left	[	[the word
Move right	]	] the word
Center	] [	] the word [
Align vertically	‖	‖ the word ‖ the word
Align horizontally, straighten type	=	the <u>word</u>
Wrong font	(wf)	th(e) word
Broken type	x	th(e) word

Searching the Web

Searching the Web using a standard search engine, such as Google, Yahoo, A9, or Answers.com, is similar to searching an electronic library catalog, but the massive amounts of information that such a search returns can be overwhelming. Knowing how to limit a search and how to winnow the results is critical in order to use the Web productively.

The first step is to search for exactly the information you need. Searching for a phrase or series of keywords is more likely to return useful links than searching on one broad term. A Google search for "pesticides," for example, brings up over forty million links. A search for "agricultural pesticide use in Minnesota" or "pesticide farm Minnesota" brings the number of responses down below one million. While this is still far more information than you can possibly sort through, the first few pages of links are likely to have the information you need. While each search engine displays returns slightly differently, the most relevant are likely to be listed first. If the website or information you want does not appear in the first few pages of links, you should probably reword your search and try again.

If you search for a phrase enclosed in quotation marks, the search engine will search for that exact string of characters within a website. This can be especially helpful when you are looking for a proper name, song lyrics or the text of a poem, or a famous phrase.

If you do not use quotation marks, the search engine will default to an "AND" search, returning only websites that contain all of the terms you enter. You can also specify an "OR" search, such as "pesticide farm Minnesota OR Wisconsin." The results will include all websites with the words "pesticide" and "farm" and either "Minnesota" or "Wisconsin." Other search options are generally available from an "Advanced Search" menu or button.

When using the Web, it is important to remember that the information you can gather is not guaranteed to be unbiased or even accurate. The information on pesticides offered by an organic farmer, for example, will likely be very different from that presented by the manufacturer of the pesticide. Be aware of the author or sponsor of any website you are using in your research, and try to cross-check any information you find on the Web.

Before making a trip to the library, try searching for books and articles online. For current newspaper articles, try using one of the many news searches such as news.google.com. If you know what article you want, check the publication's website. Almost every major periodical (magazine, journal, and newspaper) has a website with searchable archives. Though most of these websites require subscriptions for full access to their archives, many offer individual articles for a small fee.

If you wish to search multiple publications at once, see if you can get access to one of the major online databases such as LexisNexis. Almost all of these require a subscription and some are only available through school and college libraries. LexisNexis has newspapers and magazine articles, as well as legal, corporate, academic, and government documents. JSTOR and Project MUSE have large collections of journals and other scholarly publications.

Many books can also be found online. There are numerous book databases, such as Google Books, that allow full-text searches of thousands of texts. For books still under copyright, only a small excerpt containing the search term is viewable unless the book is purchased. Books in the public domain are usually available in their entirety. The following websites have searchable collections of books: books.google.com, A9.com, gutenberg.org, etext.virginia.edu.

The library catalog

The catalog is the best tool for finding books in the library. The catalog includes a separate database record for each holding in the library, whether a book, magazine or journal, videotape, audiotape, DVD or CD, map, microfilm, or other material. The information in this record will help you find the material in the library, and will also help you to decide if it will be helpful to your research.

No matter where a book is situated in the library, the catalog will direct you to it. Librarians in the United States usually organize books by one of two systems: the Dewey Decimal System or the Library of Congress System. Both systems classify books into major fields of knowledge and are explained in the section *Organization of the Library,* beginning on page 224. Thus, mathematics books will be in one section, history books in another, and so on. Within each broad area of knowledge, there are subdivisions. While these systems create an orderly arrangement for the library, without the catalog it would be very difficult for the average individual to find specific books.

Since about 1980 (in some cases earlier), libraries have been gradually converting their cataloging systems from cards to computers. Now, almost all library catalogs are fully computerized. Many catalogs are accessible over the Internet as well. If you have a computer with an Internet connection, you can search the catalog ahead of time, and go to the library only if it has the resources you need. There may be items in the library that are not in the computer catalog, however. If you are searching for older materials, you may want to ask a librarian whether there are items that have not yet been entered into the computer catalog.

There are many types of cataloging software in use, but they all share the same basic features. Because database records can hold far more information than the index cards they replaced, you can more easily tell if a book or other holding is going to be useful for your research. For more details on what you can find in the catalog record, see *What the Records Tell You,* below. Another advantage of the computer catalog is searchability. The database can be searched and ordered in many ways, allowing you to find related subjects and holdings easily.

What the records tell you. The records in the catalog database are designed to direct you to the books, but there is more information that can be learned from the records themselves.

In the first place, a record in the catalog tells you that the book you want is in the library's collection, and it may tell you if someone else has the book out on loan or if it is otherwise unavailable. The record will also let you know whether the book may be borrowed or must be used in the library. In some cases, one copy of a book is noncirculating, but another copy of the same book may be taken out on loan. The catalog record will also tell you how many copies of a book the library owns.

Other items that may be learned from a catalog record are the author's full name, date of birth, and date of death, and the title and subtitle, copyright date, date of first publication (if the book is a revision or new edition), number of pages, and publisher of the book. The record will also include the full Cataloging in Publication (CIP) data for the book. This is the bibliographic record created by the Library of Congress for a book prior to its publication. From this you can learn whether the book has illustrations, a bibliography, or an index. The CIP data also lists all the subjects under which the book is cataloged. This information can be very helpful for referring you to related subjects by which you can search the catalog further.

The most important thing that you can learn from the record is the book's call number, which will direct you to the shelf on which the book can be found. The call number will be classified by the Dewey Decimal System or the Library of Congress System (see *Organization of the Library,* page 224). Some books may have no call number. For instance, works of fiction—especially contemporary fiction—are often arranged by the author's last name in a separate fiction section, and the fiction records may have *Fic* or *F* in the space where one would normally find the call number. Some libraries may use the author's last name as the call number for fiction records. Biographies may also be treated as a separate category in some libraries. The call number on a biography may be simply *B* or *Bio* followed by the first initial of the last name of the person about whom the book is written. Thus, a biography about Sigmund Freud would have *B F* (or *Bio F*) where the call number would normally appear, while a biography by Sigmund Freud about Woodrow Wilson would have *B W* (or *Bio W*) for the call number. For holdings that are not books, the call number will specify the medium, such as *CD* or *Video.*

In addition to containing information on full works, the catalog may help you find short novels. Usually, though, it will not help you find short stories, poems, plays, essays, and other short works published in collections or anthologies. To find these you need to use reference books or a computerized index.

Organization of the catalog. Displays of lists in the catalog are alphabetized word by word. That means that when viewed as a listing, all entries beginning, for example, with the word *New* will be placed before the entries beginning with *News* or *Newton.* Thus the order will be

New astronomy theories	Newark
New Jersey	Newport
New mathematics	News
New ports	News gathering
New theories of science	Newton, Isaac
New York	Newtonian physics

The word-by-word method of alphabetizing differs from the method used by dictionaries. In dictionaries, each word or phrase is alphabetized as if it were written as one word. In a dictionary system, *Newark* would come before *New Jersey* and *New York.*

In most catalogs, abbreviations are listed as if they were spelled out. Thus, *Mt.* would be listed as if spelled *mount* and *St.* would be listed as if spelled *saint. Mc* and *M* would be listed as if spelled *Mac.* Articles (*a, an, the*) are not considered if they appear at the beginning of a title. (*The House of the Seven Gables* would be alphabetized at *House*, not at *The.*)

Using the computer catalog. Every library you visit may have different cataloging software. All systems will have a general help screen to get you started, but if you are having trouble with a particular program, ask a librarian for assistance. Although the look and navigation methods may differ, the basics of searching the computer catalog are the same.

You can search the database within a field, such as *Author, Title,* or *Subject,* or you can search for a keyword, a word or phrase that appears within any of the fields. Most programs also have advanced search features that allow you to search other fields (such as the call number) or in several fields at once to refine your search (e.g., searching for both an author and a title, which should narrow the search to the exact book for which you are looking).

Most programs will have a beginning screen with a box for entering text and a group of icons or a menu from which to select your search fields. Enter your search term into the text box, and then either click the appropriate icon or select your search type from the menu. The computer will then bring up either a list of holdings or an alphabetical list of subject categories with your search term highlighted. Select the holding you want in order to get to the complete database record. If your original search term was broad, you may go through several screens of listings. If there are too many entries to list on one page, there will be a *Next* or *More* button to click to proceed to the next screen.

If you enter an author's name, for example (using the form Last Name, First Name), and click on *Author*, the computer will return a list of every holding in the library by that author. If you search on a subject, however, the computer may return a list of holdings, or it may instead show you an alphabetical list of subjects from which you can choose the one that is most appropriate. A *Subject* search on "pesticides," for example, might return a list including several subcategories, such as "Pesticides and wildlife, Pesticides—Environmental aspects, Pesticides industry." There may be a number next to the listing showing how many items are listed under that subject category in the catalog. If there is only one listing, there may be an icon showing whether the holding is a book, or audio-visual or other material.

While the catalog can lead you to the books and allow you to eliminate some sources as irrelevant to your research, it is only a starting point. Once you have narrowed your list of possible sources, you must examine the holdings themselves to determine whether they will be useful. In addition, when you are scanning the shelves to find the sources you have already identified, you may well discover other useful books that were missed in your catalog search. Most electronic library catalogs are available over the Internet.

Using the card catalog. Although most libraries have electronically cataloged all of their holdings, some are still using card catalogs, especially for older books and other materials. The following is a brief explanation of how to use the card catalog.

What exactly is a card catalog? A card catalog is an index of (mostly) books, arranged alphabetically on three- by five-inch cards in a set of file drawers. Each file drawer is usually labeled to show what portion of the alphabet it contains. The cards list the following information about the books: author, title, and the subject or subjects covered in the book. Some cards give cross-references to other cards. A few cards are information cards: these do not direct you to a particular book but instead tell you where to find cards or items that may be hard to locate.

There are three kinds of cards in a card catalog: author cards, title cards, and subject cards. All contain the same basic information but are filed alphabetically under the author, title, or subject of the book. In some libraries, all three are interfiled in one alphabetical span; in others, the subject cards are filed separately.

Author cards. Librarians consider the author card to be the basic catalog card. The author can be one individual but could also be several people, a committee, a foundation, a magazine, or even the government.

The author card lists the author's name, last name first. On the line below, it lists the title of the book. If there are ten books in the library by one author, there will be ten author cards, one for each book. Those cards will be listed alphabetically by their titles.

Other information listed on these cards may include the publisher and date of publication, the author's birth and death dates, the number of pages, and whether or not the book contains illustrations. At the bottom of the card are the "tracings," or cataloging data. These may include other subjects under which the book is classified, some of which may be helpful in your research. The most important information is the call number, which tells you where the book is shelved. It is printed in the upper left-hand corner of the card.

Some authors do not write under their own names. The library may list the book at the pseudonym or at the real name. When you look up an author, look under the name that you are familiar with. The card catalog will clarify the name and the spelling that the library uses.

Title cards. On the title card, the title is usually typed in above the author's name. Below, the author's name is given and the title is repeated. A title card is really the basic author card with the title shown at the top.

If you know the title of a book but don't know who wrote it, the card catalog can help you find it. Titles, like authors, are listed in the card catalog in word-by-word alphabetical order.

The main thing to remember when looking for a title card is to ignore the article at the beginning of the title. Look for *A Tale of Two Cities* at *Tale*, not *A*. Look for *The Uses of Enchantment* at *Uses*, not *The*.

Some books—such as reference books—have no official author since they are compiled by several individuals. These books can be located by title.

Subject cards. Most researchers find that the subject cards are the most useful cards in the catalog. Some cards will refer you to books that cover a broad subject, and other cards will refer to books on subdivisions of a subject. There may also be an information card that leads you to related topics. Like the title card, the subject card is the same as the basic author card but with the subject in capital letters at the top of the card. There are also cross-reference cards which can lead you to other related subjects. These other subjects may or may not be useful in your research, but you should make note of any subjects that may help.

In very complicated situations, an information card will often clarify matters. For example, there are many kings named Henry from many countries. There are also people whose last names are Henry. How do you figure out which comes first? An informational card will usually explain the order used in the catalog.

Organization of the library

Today there are two organizational systems for libraries in the United States: the Dewey Decimal System and the Library of Congress System. When you enter a library, see if the books have Dewey Decimal call numbers (e.g., 792.42) or Library of Congress call numbers (e.g., PN 1993.5). Research and university libraries almost always use the Library of Congress System. Public libraries may use either system.

Call numbers stand for certain categories. The categories in the Dewey Decimal System differ from the categories in the Library of Congress System.

Dewey Decimal System. Call numbers in this system begin with Arabic numerals.

000	Generalities—bibliographies, encyclopedias, libraries, and the like
100	Philosophy and related disciplines
200	Religion
300	Social sciences—statistics, sociology, economics, law, education, and similar disciplines
400	Language—linguistics, other languages
500	Pure sciences—mathematics, astronomy, physics, chemistry, earth science, biological science, botany, zoology, and similar disciplines
600	Technology—medicine, engineering, agriculture, domestic science, business, and similar disciplines
700	The arts—architecture, sculpture, drawing, painting, photography, music, and recreational arts
800	Literature and rhetoric—American and English literature, literature from other languages
900	General geography, history, biography, and similar disciplines

Each category is subdivided further (e.g., 401, 426, 492) and decimal numbers may be added to make further distinctions (e.g., 426.12, 792.42). On the shelf, all the books are arranged in numerical order. Books without the decimal are arranged before books with the decimal, as in the series 792, 792.12, 792.3, 792.42.

Library of Congress System. Call numbers in this system begin with letters.

A	General works
B	Philosophy, psychology, and religion
C	Auxiliary sciences of history
D	History and topography (except America)
E&F	America
G	Geography, anthropology, and recreation
H	Social sciences
J	Political science
K	Law
L	Education
M	Music

N	Fine arts
P	Language and literature
Q	Science
R	Medicine
S	Agriculture
T	Technology
U	Military science
V	Naval science
Z	Bibliography, library science, and information resources

Note that the letters I, O, W, X, and Y are not included. They may some day be used if further categories become necessary. Categories in the Library of Congress System are further subdivided with a second letter, then a numeral of one to four digits, then a decimal followed by a numeral or a letter and a numeral. Sometimes there is a further subdivision of categories introduced by a second decimal.

On the shelf, books are arranged alphabetically by letter category, as in P, PN, PS. Within each of the letter categories, books are arranged in numerical order from 1 to 9999, as in PN1, PN86, PN1993, PN1993.5, PN1994, PN6110.

Indexes and bibliographies

Indexes to newspapers and periodicals. An index is a guide to direct you to material on a subject or by an author. Using an index involves two processes. The first is finding out whether and where an article has been published. The second process is sometimes more difficult—finding a copy of the required newspaper or magazine. Large libraries may have bound volumes of periodicals and microfilm or microfiche copies of newspapers. Most magazines prepare an annual alphabetical list of the articles they've published during the year. For recent articles, this process is fairly simple. Newspapers and journals that publish electronic versions also archive their articles online. These archives can be reached from the website of the journal or newspaper. Most articles published before the rise of online journalism are unlikely to be available in these archives, however.

The Readers' Guide to Periodical Literature, available in print and online through WilsonWeb, directs you to articles in the most widely read magazines in the United States. Regular supplements (for the print edition) are available to bring you up to date. *Access* (J.G. Burke Publishers) indexes many periodicals not indexed in *Readers' Guide*.

Indexes to direct you to more specialized journals in particular fields are also available. A short list of examples includes

- *Applied Science and Technology Index*
- *Art Index*
- *Biological and Agricultural Index*
- *Business Periodicals Index*
- *Cumulative Book Index*
- *Education Index*
- *Humanities Index*
- *Index to Legal Periodicals*
- *Music Index*
- *Social Science Index*
- *Ulrich's International Periodical Index* (Lists the names of periodicals in many languages. It does not index specific articles.)

Many of these are also available online, through WilsonWeb, Thomson Gale, or Proquest. While all of these companies charge for access, a university or research library may have a subscription that patrons can use.

Until the advent of electronic publishing, very few newspapers were indexed. It may be possible to find information on world or national events before the 1990s in one of the following newspaper indexes:

- *Index to the Christian Science Monitor*
- *The New York Times Index*
- *The Times Index, London*
- *The Newspaper Index* (Indexes a few large American newspapers.)

If your library has the material to which the indexes refer, it is probably on microfilm or microfiche.

These indexes are now available online, and the articles are sometimes available as well. More recent articles from these newspapers should be fully archived and available through the newspaper's website or from a database site such as WilsonWeb or Proquest. Smaller newspapers also often archive their online editions, but articles published before the newspaper was published electronically are unlikely to have been added to the archive. Local newspapers vary greatly in their manner of filing material about old stories and in their willingness to let people not on staff use the files. Libraries may still have microfilm or microfiche collections of older newspapers, however.

Indexes to material shorter than book length. Short works are difficult to locate. They generally come in anthologies, and anthology titles do not necessarily indicate what specific works they contain. If you want to find a poem, short story, play, or essay, you may find the relevant anthology or anthologies by using an index or by searching on the World Wide Web. All of the following indexes are available online and in print, except for Ottemiller's, which is available only in print, and Inter-Play, which is available only online.

For poetry:

- *Granger's Index to Poetry* (Poems are listed by author, first line, title, and subject.)

For short stories:

- *Short Story Index* (Short stories are indexed by author, title, and subject. Some periodicals are included, as well as anthologies.)

For essays:

- *Essays and General Literature Index* (Essays and literary criticism are indexed by author and subject.)

For plays:

- *Inter-Play* (Online index to plays originally published in collections, anthologies, and periodicals; various languages; late 19th century to present.)
- *Ottemiller's Index to Plays in Collections, 1900–1975* (Plays are indexed by author and title.)

- *Play Index* (Organized by year; each volume covers three to four years.)

Bibliographies. You can locate many bibliographies indirectly. When you find a book on a subject you are investigating, that book may have a bibliography that you can use to find further sources. No bibliography in a book will be more up-to-date than the book itself, however, so note the publication date. The following are more general sources that will help you find bibliographies:

- *Bibliography of Bibliographies* (Lists many bibliographies.)
- *Bibliographic Index* (Also a bibliography of bibliographies.)
- *Subject Guide to Books in Print* (List of American books still in print. The list is arranged by subject and may prove useful as a means of finding titles of books on a particular subject.)
- *Cumulative Books Index* (Lists English-language books by subject, author, and title.)

There are also many special-subject lists of books. A few examples are:

- *The Reader's Advisor*
- *Literary Research Guide*
- *Sources of Information in the Social Sciences*
- *Harvard Guide to American History*
- *Science and Engineering Reference Sources*

Again, most of these references are searchable over the Internet.

Government and public institutions

Try the offices of the city, town, county, or state government. There are often many maps, records, and special information bulletins available.

Chambers of commerce are often glad to supply material and answer questions about their area. They will often direct you to other people or organizations who can supply information or material that they do not have.

Government agencies of all levels have a wealth of information. It is up to you to locate the agency and to call, write, or e-mail for the information you need. Many government agencies now have websites, on which you can find addresses, phone numbers, and e-mail addresses.

The Federal Depository Library Program is a federal program to acquire and disseminate information from all three branches of the federal government. There are depository libraries in all 50 states and in some US territories; they allow free public access to the federal depository holdings. The website www.gpoaccess.gov explains the program in further depth; a search function on that page will help you find the nearest depository library.

The federal government's Government Printing Office publishes a large number of pamphlets and books on a great variety of subjects. You can get a list of all the office's publications or a list on a specific subject by writing to: Superintendent of Documents, Government Printing Office, Washington, DC 20402.

The Catalog of US Government Publications (catalog.gpo.gov) allows you to search for any federal publication, historical or current. If the publication is available online, it is directly linked to the catalog. Otherwise, it can be purchased from the GPO online bookstore (bookstore.gpo.gov). If the publication is out of print, you may still be able to find it in a Federal Depository Library.

The following publications are sources of information about the federal government. All of these, and many more GPO publications, are available from the GPO online bookstore.

- *Congressional Record* (A daily record of the activities of Congress, including indexes giving the names, subjects, and history of all bills.)
- *Federal Register* (A daily record of the activities of executive branch departments and agencies such as the Food and Drug Administration and Internal Revenue Service, including regulations, policy proposals, and public comments.)
- *Official Congressional Directory* (Published annually by the Government Printing Office, a list of the names and addresses of everyone connected with the federal government, maps of Congressional Districts, and short biographies of members of Congress.)

- *US Government Manual* (A comprehensive list of all the agencies, boards, committees, and commissions in all three branches of the federal government, published annually.)

Basic reference works and Internet resources

Encyclopedias. Encyclopedias provide good background material. They are a fine place to begin research on many topics. Often, an encyclopedia provides a short bibliography as well.

There are two kinds of encyclopedias—general and special purpose. Either kind may be organized alphabetically or by subject. Here are some examples of general encyclopedias:

- *Collier's Encyclopedia*
- *The Columbia Encyclopedia, Sixth Edition*
- *Compton's Encyclopedia and Fact-Index*
- *Encyclopædia Britannica*
- *Encyclopedia Americana*
- *Wikipedia.com*

When it comes to special-purpose reference books, it can be hard to draw the line between encyclopedias and dictionaries. Both should be consulted (see the next section) if both exist in a special field. Here are some examples of special-purpose encyclopedias:

- *Encyclopedia of Computer Science and Engineering*
- *A Handbook to Literature* by William Harmon and C. Hugh Holman
- *The International Cyclopedia of Music and Musicians*
- *McGraw-Hill Encyclopedia of Science and Technology*
- *The New Princeton Encyclopedia of Poetry and Poetics*
- *The Oxford Companion to World Sports and Games*
- *The Routledge Encyclopedia of Philosophy*
- *The Stanford Encyclopedia of Philosophy*
- *Walker's Mammals of the World*

Dictionaries. General dictionaries contain information such as definitions, pronunciations, synonyms, and word histories. You can access many of these dictionaries through libraryspot.com and bartleby.com. Here are some examples of useful general dictionaries:

- *The American Heritage® Dictionary of the English Language, Fourth Edition*
- *The American Heritage® College Dictionary, Fourth Edition*
- *Merriam-Webster's Collegiate Dictionary, Eleventh Edition*
- *The New Oxford American Dictionary*
- *Random House Webster's College Dictionary*
- *Random House Webster's Unabridged Dictionary*
- *Webster's New World Dictionary of the American Language*
- *Webster's Third New International Dictionary, Unabridged*

For slang:

- *Historical Dictionary of American Slang*, edited by J. E. Lighter (Multiple volumes, unfinished.)
- *Dictionary of American Slang, Third Edition* by Robert Chapman
- *A Dictionary of Slang and Unconventional English* by Eric Partridge

For pronunciations:

- *A Pronouncing Dictionary of American English* by John S. Kenyon and Thomas A. Knott

For synonyms:

- *The American Heritage® College Thesaurus*
- *Merriam-Webster's Collegiate Thesaurus*
- *Random House Roget's College Thesaurus*
- *Roget's International Thesaurus, Sixth Edition*
- *Webster's New Dictionary of Synonyms*
- *Webster's New World Roget's A–Z Thesaurus*

For word background and historical usages:

- *The American Heritage® Dictionary of Indo-European Roots, Second Edition*, by Calvert Watkins
- *Chambers Dictionary of Etymology* by Robert K. Barnhart
- *A Dictionary of Americanisms on Historical Principles* by M. M. Mathews

- *An Etymological Dictionary of the English Language* by Walter William Skeat
- *Hobson-Jobson: The Anglo-Indian Dictionary* by Henry Yule and A. C. Burnell
- *Oxford Dictionary of English Etymology* by C. T. Onions
- *The Oxford English Dictionary* (often called *the OED*)

Concordances to the Bible, to Shakespeare, and to other works will help you find specific uses of words within the works. A concordance is a book that lists all the words used in a particular book and indicates exactly where each word is used each time it is used.

It is often hard to draw the line between encyclopedias and dictionaries when it comes to special-purpose items. The following are a few examples of special-purpose dictionaries:

- *Academic Press Dictionary of Science and Technology*
- *The American Heritage® Science Dictionary*
- *The American Political Dictionary*
- *Black's Law Dictionary*
- *A Comprehensive Dictionary of Psychological and Psychoanalytic Terms*
- *Dictionary of American History*
- *Dictionary of American Regional English* (DARE)
- *Dictionary of Architectural Science*
- *Dictionary of the Bible*
- *A Dictionary of Classical Antiquities*
- *A Dictionary of Comparative Religion*
- *Dictionary of Education*
- *A Dictionary of the Social Sciences*
- *Dorland's Illustrated Medical Dictionary*
- *The Harvard Dictionary of Music*
- *McGraw-Hill Dictionary of Scientific and Technical Terms*
- *The New Grove's Dictionary of Music and Musicians*
- *The American Heritage® Medical Dictionary*
- *Webster's Sports Dictionary*

English usage. There are many books available on grammar and writing. The following are among the best:

- *The American Heritage® Guide to Contemporary Usage and Style*
- *The Careful Writer* by Theodore M. Bernstein
- *A Dictionary of Contemporary American Usage* by Bergen Evans and Cornelia Evans
- *A Dictionary of Modern English Usage* by H. W. Fowler
- *The Elements of Style, Fourth Edition,* by Strunk and White
- *Garner's Modern American Usage* by Bryan A. Garner
- *Harper Dictionary of Contemporary Usage* by William Morris and Mary Morris
- *Merriam-Webster's Dictionary of English Usage*
- *Modern American Usage* by Wilson Follett
- *On Writing Well* by William Zinsser

Editing and printing. Consult the following for information on editing, copyediting, preparing manuscripts, book publication, and similar topics:

- *American Medical Association Manual of Style, Ninth Edition*
- *The Chicago Manual of Style, Fifteenth Edition,* The University of Chicago Press
- *Manual for Writers of Term Papers, Theses, and Dissertations, Sixth Edition,* by Kate L. Turabian
- *MLA Style Manual and Guide to Scholarly Publishing, Second Edition,* by Joseph Gibaldi
- *Publication Manual of the American Psychological Association, Fifth Edition*
- *Style Manual of the United States Government Printing Office*

Research guides. The following book-length guides to research contain in-depth explanations of the research process.

- *The Craft of Research, Second Edition,* by Wayne C. Booth, Joseph M. Williams, and Gregory G. Colomb
- *The Modern Researcher, Fifth Edition,* by Jacques Barzun and Henry F. Graff

Biographical references. There are many reference books that contain brief, condensed facts and dates about people. If you are not sure which book to look at, try one from the following list:

- *Biography Almanac*
- *Biography and Genealogy Master-Index*
- *Biography Index*

Below are some of the more popular biographical reference books:

- *Chambers Biographical Dictionary*
- *Current Biography*
- *Dictionary of American Biography*
- *Dictionary of Canadian Biography*
- *Dictionary of National Biography* (for British history)
- *The International Who's Who*
- *The McGraw-Hill Encyclopedia of World Biography*
- *Merriam-Webster's Biographical Dictionary*
- *Who's Who*
- *Who's Who in America*
- *Who's Who in the World*
- *Who Was Who in America*

In addition, there are many specialized *Who's Who* books that are regional or professional in scope. There are also books of biographies of authors, scientists, and other types of professionals—for example, Asimov's *Biographical Encyclopedia of Science and Technology.* Short biographies can also be found in encyclopedias and in dictionaries of specialized fields.

Maps and atlases. Atlases may contain maps of the modern world, of the world during particular historical periods, or of extraterrestrial locations.

For contemporary maps:

- *Atlas of the Moon*, by Antonin Rukl
- *Goode's World Atlas*, Rand McNally
- *Google Earth*
- *The Great World Atlas*, Dorling-Kindersley
- *Hammond World Atlas*
- *National Geographic Atlas of the World*
- *Oxford Atlas of the World*
- *Rand McNally New International Atlas*
- *The Times Atlas of the World*

For historical maps:

- *The Atlas of African-American History and Politics*, McGraw-Hill
- *Atlas of American History*
- *Atlas of the Classical World*
- *Hammond Atlas of World History*
- *National Geographic Historical Atlas of the United States*
- *Oxford Atlas of World History*
- *Historical Atlas of the World*, Hammond

There are a variety of other sources from which you can obtain maps. The Automobile Association of America makes maps available to members, the National Geographic Society prepares both contemporary maps and historical maps, and Rand McNally, Hammond, and other companies publish books of maps as well as individual maps. In addition, travel agencies, foreign consultants, chambers of commerce, and other organizations may offer maps. Online maps are the most current.

Secretarial handbooks. Information about office procedures and skills can be found in these books:

Complete Secretary's Handbook by Mary A. DeVries
Elements of Business Writing by Gary Blake and Robert W. Bly
The Gregg Reference Manual by William A. Sabin
Merriam-Webster's Secretarial Handbook, Third Edition
The New Office Professional's Handbook, Fourth Edition, Houghton Mifflin
The Secretary's Handbook by Sarah Augusta Taintor and Kate M. Monro, edited by Margaret D. Shertzer
Webster's New World Office Professional's Handbook, Macmillan

Parliamentary procedure. For rules governing parliamentary procedure, consult the following:

- *Robert's Rules of Order*
- *Sturgis Standard Code of Parliamentary Procedure* by Alice F. Sturgis

Document anthologies. If you need to find the text of the Magna Carta or George Washington's Farewell Address, or if you are doing research using primary sources, the best place to look is online. Some museums have some portion of their collections online, and many universities collect and allow online access to historical documents as well. Here are some sites that may help:

- memory.loc.gov—Library of Congress American Memory Collection; documents and other archival material from US history
- www.bl.uk—The British Library
- www.ourdocuments.gov—100 milestone documents in US history
- www.perseus.tufts.edu—The Perseus Digital Library; texts for research in the humanities
- www.yale.edu/lawweb/avalon—The Avalon Project at Yale Law School; documents in law, history, and diplomacy

Books of quotations. Some books offer well-known quotations:

- *Contemporary Quotations* by James B. Simpson (after 1950)
- *Bartlett's Familiar Quotations, Seventeenth Edition,* by John Bartlett and Justin Kaplan
- *Home Book of Quotations* by Burton E. Stevenson
- *The International Thesaurus of Quotations, Revised Edition,* by Eugene Ehrlich
- *Oxford Dictionary of Quotations* by Elizabeth Knowles

Others offer quotations on certain subjects or from certain groups of people:

- *Leo Rosten's Treasury of Jewish Quotations*
- *My Soul Looks Back, 'Less I Forget: A Collection of Quotations by People of Color* by D. Winbush Riley
- *The New Beacon Book of Quotations by Women* by Rosalie Maggio
- *The Oxford Dictionary of Humorous Quotations* by Ned Sherrin

Company and market information. All public companies and many private companies file reports with the US Securities and Exchange Commission (SEC). These filings contain essential financial information about the company. The most important document is the annual report (form 10-K), which details the company's performance over the past year. SEC filings are available free of charge through the SEC website sec.gov and at secinfo.com. In addition, most companies post their annual reports on their website.

For news and research reports about companies:

- hoovers.com
- reuters.com

For market data including historical prices:

- finance.yahoo.com

For currency data:

- oanda.com

Demographic and economic data. Government websites are the best place to find US statistics. Start with fedstats.gov, which has links to all the federal agencies that publish statistics.

For US census data:

- census.gov
- fisher.lib.virginia.edu/collections/stats/histcensus—University of Virginia historical census browser

For US economic data:

- economicindicators.gov
- export.gov
- federalreserve.gov
- stats.bls.gov

Most foreign governments also have websites with economic and demographic statistics. In addition, international organizations such as the United Nations (un.org), the World Bank (worldbank.org), and the International Monetary Fund (imf.org) have large statistical databases that include almost every country in the world. For brief country profiles, visit the CIA's World Factbook at cia.gov/cia/publications/factbook/index.html.

INDEX

abbreviations
  capitalizing, 6
  in card catalogs, 221
  numbers and, 38
  in papers and reports, 200
  plurals, forming, 31
  punctuating, 22
absolute construction, in phrases and verb forms, 68
abstract nouns, 39
abstracts, in papers and reports, 194
academic degrees. *See* address, forms of
acknowledgments page, 193–194
acronyms, style guide for, 6
active voice, 47, 57
address, forms of
  academic titles, 160–161
  men, 158
  officials and dignitaries, 158–159
  spouses, 158
  style guide for, 4–5
  table, 160–178
  women, 157–158
addresses, 38, 143. *See also* inside address
adjectives. *See also* compound adjectives
  grammar rules for, 50–51
  hyphens and, 15
  subject/predicate, modifying, 55, 56
  verb forms as, 66–67
adverbs
  compound adjectives and, 33
  grammar rules for, 50, 51, 55
aircraft names, style guide for, 4, 7
all-, use of, 14
AM and *PM,* use of, 38
AMA style (American Medical Association), 205, 206, 211
and, use of, 49
animal names, style guide for, 30–31
antecedents, avoiding unclear, 45
anthologies, document, 237
APA style (American Psychological Association), 205, 206, 209–210
apostrophes, use of, 16, 37, 41
apposition
  phrases in, 66
  pronouns and, 44
  punctuation, 18
artistic works, style guide for, 5, 7
astronomical terms, style guide for, 6
atlases, research guide to, 235–236
attention line, in business letters, 139, 143–144
author cards, in library catalogs,

guide for, 3–4, 6, 19
gerunds
in compound nouns, 8
as nouns, 67
pronouns and, 43
glossary, in papers and reports, 201
government agencies, research guide to, 229–231
government officials. *See* address, forms of
grammar, 39, 75–76, 233–234. *See also* parts of speech; sentences
greeting line. *See* salutations
guidewords, in memos and e-mail, 151, 154–156

half-, use of, 14
headings
in business letters, 145
in fax cover sheets, 153
in memos and e-mail, 151
in papers and reports, 194–196, 198
high- and *low-*, in compound modifiers, 9, 33
historical periods/events, style guide for, 3, 6
holidays, style guide for, 5
homographs, 32
honorary titles. *See* address, forms of
hyphens, use of
compound modifiers, 9–11, 33
measurements, 12–13
numbers, 12–13, 37
other uses, 14–15
phrases, 11
prefixes, 13–14
proper names, 12

word compounding and, 8, 9, 31–34

i, words ending in, 30
Ibid., use of, 201
"*ie*," spelling rules for, 28
illustrations, in papers and reports, 193, 197–199
imperative mood, of a verb, 47, 48
imperative sentences, 71–72
indefinite pronouns, 42, 44
independent clauses, 60, 61–62, 63
index cards, use of, 182, 183, 202
indexes
in papers and reports, 202–204
research guide to, 226–229
indicative mood, of a verb, 47
indirect objects, 40, 56
indirect questions, 70–71
informal writing
numbers in, 32, 37–38
papers and reports, 190, 191
information cards, 183–184, 187–188
In re, use of, 145
inside address, 139, 142–143, 157. *See also* address, forms of
Internet, the. *See* online searches
interrogative
adverbs, 51
pronouns, 42
sentences, 70
interviews, job, 138
intransitive verbs, 45, 46, 54
irregular
adjectives, 50
adverbs, 51